6-20-74
16:39

D1607903

Pittsburgh Series in Bibliography

EDITORIAL BOARD

Matthew J. Bruccoli, General Editor

William R. Cagle

Charles W. Mann

Joel Myerson

RAYMOND CHANDLER

Alfred A. Knopf, Inc.

Raymond Chandler

A DESCRIPTIVE BIBLIOGRAPHY

Matthew J. Bruccoli

UNIVERSITY OF
PITTSBURGH PRESS
1979

CENTRAL MISSOURI
STATE UNIVERSITY
Warrensburg,
Missouri

Published by the University of Pittsburgh Press, Pittsburgh, Pa. 15260
Copyright © 1979, University of Pittsburgh Press
All rights reserved
Feffer and Simons, Inc., London
Manufactured in the United States of America

Library of Congress Cataloging in Publication Data

Bruccoli, Matthew Joseph, 1931–
    Raymond Chandler.

    (Pittsburgh series in bibliography)
    Includes index.
    1.   Chandler, Raymond, 1888–1959—Bibliography.
I.   Series.
Z8159.15.B763   [PS3505.H3224]   016.813'5'2   78-4280
ISBN 0-8229-3382-9

PS
3505
.H3224
Z526
1979

Once Again
to
Fraze

Contents

Acknowledgments

ANY good bibliography is a collaboration between the compiler and all the librarians, researchers, collectors, publishers, bookdealers, and others who assisted him. This bibliography would have been impossible without their help: Virginia Ashley, Mary Bruccoli, William R. Cagle, C. E. Frazer Clark, Jr., Ashbell Green, Helga Greene, Muriel Hamilton, David Harris, Robert G. Hayman, Dean Keller, Hyman W. Kritzer, Clifford McCarty, Roger Machell, Frank MacShane, Charles W. Mann, Walker Martin, Neil Morgan, William Nolan, Elizabeth Pugh, Jean Rhyne, Anthony Rota, Kathrine Sorley Walker, Joyce Werner, Brooke Whiting, and J. F. Whitt. The staffs of the Cooper Library of the University of South Carolina, The Library of Congress, The British Library, the Bodleian Library, the Kent State University Library, the UCLA Library, and the U.S. Copyright Office were particularly helpful among the many institutions which were of assistance.

I am greatly indebted to Louise Craft, the editor in charge of the Pittsburgh Series in Bibliography, who labored over my typescript. Richard Taylor, University of South Carolina Information Services, did the photographic work cheerfully and competently. Karen Rood checked every entry, made the index, and substantially improved this bibliography. Cara White is the best secretary in the world. The Pittsburgh Series in Bibliography would not exist without the support of Frederick A. Hetzel, Director of the University of Pittsburgh Press.

Many people at the University of South Carolina have been generous with help. Provost Keith Davis arranged for a Shell Travel Grant. Dr. William Nolte, Head of the Department of English, provided research and travel assistance.

I am grateful that I am at the University of South Carolina where I can get my work done.

Introduction

PUBLICATION is the essential act of scholarship, but all bibliographies are works in progress.

FORMAT

Section A lists chronologically all books and pamphlets by Raymond Chandler—including all printings of all editions in English. At the end of this section there is an AA supplemental list of collections of Chandler's writing. The numbering system for Section A designates the edition and printing for each entry. Thus for *The Big Sleep, A 1.15.a* indicates that it is the first book published by Chandler (*A 1*), and that the entry describes the fifteenth edition (*15*), first printing (*a*).

Section B lists chronologically all titles in which material by Chandler appears for the first time in a book. Usually the first printings only of these items are described.

Section C lists chronologically all first appearances of Chandler's work in magazines and newspapers—including interviews.

Section D describes one Chandler keepsake.

Section E lists blurbs by Chandler on dust jackets of books by other authors.

Section F lists chronologically screenplays by Chandler—both produced and unproduced. It includes a section of motion pictures made from Chandler's books.

Appendix 1 contains the compiler's notes.

Appendix 2 lists the principal works about Chandler.

TERMS AND METHODS

Edition. All the copies of a book printed from a single setting of type—including all reprintings from standing type, from plates, or by photo-offset.

Printing. All the copies of a book printed at one time (without removing the type or plates from the press). Printings exist within editions.

No *states* or *issues* have been noted for Chandler's books.

Edition and *printing* have been restricted to the sheets of the book. Binding or dust-jacket variants have no bearing on these terms.[1] Binding variants in this bibliography are treated simply as binding variants.

---

1. This statement holds for twentieth-century publishing. It is not possible to be so dogmatic for nineteenth-century publishing, when parts of a printing were marketed in different formats—

The form of entry for first English editions or printings is somewhat condensed from the full form provided for American editions, except when the English edition precedes the American.

Dust jackets for Section A entries have been described in detail because they are part of the original publication effort and sometimes provide information about how the book was marketed. There is, of course, no certainty that a jacket now on a copy of a book was always on it.

For binding-cloth designations I have used the method proposed by Tanselle;[2] most of these cloth grains are illustrated in Jacob Blanck, ed., *The Bibliography of American Literature* (New Haven: Yale University Press, 1955–).

Color specifications are taken from the *ISCC-NBS Color Name Charts Illustrated with Centroid Colors* (National Bureau of Standards).[3] A color designation holds for subsequent lines unless a color change is stipulated.

The spines of bindings or dust jackets are printed horizontally unless otherwise stipulated. The reader is to assume that vertically printed spines read from top to bottom, unless otherwise stipulated.

In the descriptions of title pages, bindings, and dust jackets, the color of the lettering is always black, unless otherwise stipulated. The type is roman, unless otherwise stipulated.

The term *perfect binding* refers to books in which the pages are held together with adhesive along the back edge after the folds have been trimmed off—for example, most paperbacks.

Dates provided within brackets do not appear on the title pages. Usually—but not invariably—they are taken from the copyright page.

The descriptions do not include leaf thickness or sheet bulk because there is no case for Chandler in which these measurements are required to differentiate printings.

Location symbols:

BL: British Library, London
BOD: Bodleian Library, Oxford
Kent: Kent State University Library
LC: Library of Congress
Lilly: Lilly Library, Indiana University
MJB: Collection of Matthew J. Bruccoli

For paperbacks, the serial number provided is that of the first printing. Paperback publishers normally change the serial number in later printings, but this information has not been noted in this bibliography.

---

e.g., cloth, paper, and two-in-one bindings. In such cases it is difficult to avoid calling the different bindings *issues* because they do represent a deliberate attempt to alter the condition of publication.

2. G. Thomas Tanselle, "The Specifications of Binding Cloth," *The Library*, 21 (September 1966), 246–247.

3. G. Thomas Tanselle, "A System of Color Identification for Bibliographical Description," *Studies in Bibliography*, 20 (1967), 203–204. The compiler suspects that the use of the Centroid designations gives a false sense of precision. Oxidation and fading make exact color identification difficult, if not impossible. The compiler is color-blind; the color identifications in this bibliography were made by Mary Bruccoli.

Some of the copyright pages in Chandler's American editions stipulate simultaneous Canadian publication, but most of these Canadian publications do not exist. The claim was made for copyright purposes. Canadian publications have been listed in this bibliography only when the compiler has examined them.

It is desirable in bibliographical description to avoid end-of-line hyphens in transcriptions. Because of word lengths and a measured line, however, it is impossible to satisfy this requirement. End-of-line hyphens have been avoided wherever possible, and always where a hyphen would create ambiguity.

A bibliography is outdated the day it goes to the printer. Additions and corrections are earnestly solicited.

The University of South Carolina
19 March 1977

A. Separate Publications

A 1 THE BIG SLEEP

A 1.1.a
First edition, first printing (1939)

A 1.1.a: 7³/₈″ × 4¹⁵/₁₆″

COPYRIGHT 1939 BY RAYMOND CHANDLER

All rights reserved. No part of this book may be reproduced in any form without permission in writing from the publisher, except by a reviewer who may quote brief passages in a review to be printed in a magazine or newspaper.

Manufactured in the United States of America

FIRST EDITION

Published Simultaneously in Canada by The Ryerson Press

[i–viii] [1–2] 3–277 [278–280]

[1–18]⁸

Contents: p. i: blank; p. ii: 'MYSTERY STORIES [5 titles]'; p. iii: half title; p. iv: blank; p. v: title page; p. vi: copyright page; p. vii: disclaimer; p. viii: blank; p. 1: half title; p. 2: blank; pp. 3–227: text; p. 278: '*A Note on the Type in which this Book is set*'; pp. 279–280: blank.

Typography and paper: $5^7/_{16}''$ ($5^{11}/_{16}''$) × $3^9/_{16}''$; 28 lines per page. Running heads: rectos and versos, '*the big sleep*'. Wove paper.

Binding: Brownish orange (#54) V cloth (smooth); front, back, and spine stamped in dark gray blue (#187). Front: '[within single-rule frame and oval] raymond | chandler | *the* | *big* | *sleep*'. Spine: '[2 lines in script] Raymond | Chandler | [3 lines within single-rule frame and oval] *the* | *big* | *sleep* | [line of loops] | *Alfred A Knopf* | [line of dots]'. Back: '[lower right: borzoi device] | *BORZOI*'. White endpapers. All edges trimmed. Top edge stained dark blue.

Dust jacket: Front and spine printed against red, white, and blue background. Front: '[3 lines slanting up from left to right] [dark blue outlined in white] THE | [light blue outlined in dark blue] BIG | [blue white outlined in black] SLEEP | [white script] By [white roman] RAYMOND CHANDLER'. Spine: '[white] RAYMOND | CHANDLER | [3 lines slanting up front left to right] [dark blue] THE | [light blue] BIG | [white] SLEEP | [Borzoi Books seal in red and white box] | [white] ALFRED • A • KNOPF'. Back: '[red] BORZOI MYSTERIES [6 titles in red and blue]'. Front flap: blurb. Back flap: note on Chandler.

Publication: 5,000 copies of the first printing. Published 6 February 1939. $2.00. Copyright 6 February 1939. Copyright #A125939.

Printing: Composed, printed, and bound by H. Wolff, New York City.

Locations: Kent (dj); Lilly (dj).

Review copy

First-printing sheets bound in strong yellow green (#117), stiff, printed paper wrappers.

Location: Kent.

the big sleep

Not since Dashiell Hammett first appeared has there been a murder mystery story with the power, pace, and terrifying atmosphere of this one. And like Hammett's, this is more than a "murder mystery"; it is a novel of crime and character, written with uncommon skill and in a tight, tense style which is irresistible.

The center of the plot is a family; an old, paralyzed ex-soldier, who made a fortune in oil; his two beautiful daughters—one a gambler, the other a degenerate; and a strangely missing son-in-law. Around such a family, with all its money, its vices, and its hidden scandals, it was inevitable that there should cluster blackmailers, gangsters, and purveyors of forbidden thrills. There are violence and shameful things in the family's history, but the detective—shrewd, strong, incorruptible, the healthy force amid the shadows and the whispers—who started out to break a blackmail case and ended up to his neck in a series of mysterious murders, clears the atmosphere and leaves the reader content that justice, though of an unexpected sort, will after all be done.

RAYMOND CHANDLER
THE BIG SLEEP

THE BIG SLEEP · RAYMOND CHANDLER

ALFRED·A·KNOPF

Raymond Chandler

has had that type of career which is commonly referred to as "checkered." Born in Chicago of an Irish mother and an American father, he went early to England, where eventually he attended Dulwich College. After completing his education in France and Germany, he turned first to school-teaching as a profession, but soon gave that up in favor of writing. He became successively a book-reviewer, poet, paragraph-writer, and essayist. Following the war, in which he served with the Canadian Infantry, he came to the United States, where he has been variously occupied ever since in such capacities as accountant, tax expert, oil executive, and pulp writer. *The Big Sleep* is his first novel.

BORZOI MYSTERIES

DASHIELL HAMMETT OMNIBUS
Three murder-mystery novels in one volume by the man whom Alexander Woollcott has called the greatest American detective-story writer. The works included are *Red Harvest*, *The Dain Curse*, and *The Maltese Falcon*.

THE BIG SLEEP
by Raymond Chandler
Not since Dashiell Hammett first appeared has there been a murder-mystery story with the power, pace, and terrifying atmosphere of this one. And like Hammett's, this is more than a "murder mystery"; it is a novel of crime and character, written with uncommon skill and in a tight, tense style which is irresistible.

CAUSE FOR ALARM
by Eric Ambler
This one is about Nicholas Marlow, engineer, who accepted the job of a Milan representative of an English machinery firm and immediately became entangled in a web of international intrigue and espionage. And luck, too, never abandons him and finally he succeeded in putting a kink in the Rome-Berlin axis.

FOUR FRIGHTENED WOMEN
by George Harmon Coxe
All Murdock had to do to was go down to the home of Ted Bernard, the radio comedian, and get some pictures of him and of his weekend guest, Irene Alexander, who was still one of America's movie sweethearts. The next morning the actress's body was found in her bedroom—and Murdock was one of the chief suspects. All of which makes Murdock's best case, for this time he is not just a smart newspaper man, but a man fighting to save his own skin.

TRENT INTERVENES
by E. C. Bentley
Here is Trent carrying on with his "cases" in the most casual, competent and stylish, though Mr. Bentley is too good an artist to make him invariably correct. There are a round dozen of "cases" in the collection, each one full of excitement, provocation, and final satisfaction.

THREE STAR OMNIBUS
Three great murder-mystery stories in one volume: *Trent's Last Case* by E. C. Bentley, *Green Ice* by Raoul Whitfield, and *The Middle Temple Murder* by J.S. Fletcher.

ALFRED·A·KNOPF · PUBLISHER · N.Y.

BORZOI BOOKS

Dust jacket for A1.1.a

IN **1929** WE GAVE YOU

HAMMETT

IN **1934** WE GAVE YOU

CAIN

In **1939** *we give you*

RAYMOND CHANDLER

and

The Big Sleep

WE PREDICT that THE BIG SLEEP will duplicate the success of *The Thin Man* and *The Postman Always Rings Twice*, and will promote it and advertise it accordingly.

Read this copy now for your own pleasure.

ALFRED · A · KNOPF NEW YORK · N · Y :

Front wrapper of A 1.1.a review copy

A 1.1.b
First edition, second printing: New York: Knopf, 1939.

Copyright page: 'First and Second Printing before Publication | Published February 6, 1939'.

A 1.1.c
First edition, third printing: New York: Grosset & Dunlap, 1940.

Not seen.

A 1.1.d
First edition, fourth printing: New York: Knopf, [1945].

Copyright page: 'First issued as a BLACK WIDOW THRILLER January 1945'.

$1.75.

A 1.1.e
First edition, fifth printing: New York: Knopf, 1946.

Black Widow Thriller. Not seen.

A 1.2.a
First English edition, first printing (1939)

THE BIG SLEEP

by
RAYMOND CHANDLER

HAMISH HAMILTON
90 GREAT RUSSELL STREET LONDON

A 1.2: 7¹/₄″ × 4⁷/₈″

Copyright page: 'First Published 1939 | PRINTED IN GUERNSEY, C.I., BRITISH | ISLES, BY THE STAR AND GAZETTE LTD.'

[1–10] 11–301 [302–304]

[A] B–I K–T⁸

Contents: pp. 1–2: blank; p. 3: half title; p. 4: blank; p. 5: title page; p. 6: copyright page; p. 7: disclaimer; p. 8: blank; p. 9: half title; p. 10: blank; pp. 11–302: text; pp. 303–304: blank.

Typography and paper: 5¹/₈″ (5⁵/₈″) × 3⁷/₁₆″; 29 lines per page. Running heads: rectos and versos, 'THE BIG SLEEP'. Wove paper.

Binding: Black V cloth (smooth); front, back and spine stamped in strong reddish orange (#35). Front: thick-and-thin-rules frame, with 'HH' in each corner. Spine: '[thick and thin rules] | THE | BIG | SLEEP | RAYMOND | CHANDLER | [HH device] | HAMISH | HAMILTON | [thin and thick rules]'. Back: same as front. White endpapers. All edges trimmed.

Dust jacket: Front printed against bright orange background: '[yellow] THE BIG | SLEEP | [hand holding brown revolver with white smoke coming from muzzle] | [white] RAYMOND | CHANDLER'. Spine probably printed against bright orange (only examined copy is faded): '[yellow] THE | BIG | SLEEP | [continuation of white smoke] | [white] RAYMOND | CHANDLER | HAMISH | HAMILTON'. Back printed against white background: '[black within double-rules frame] *Selected Thrillers, Spring 1939* [3 titles]'. Front flap: blurb. Back flap: blank.

Publication: Unknown number of copies of the first printing. Published March 1939. 7/6.

Printing: See copyright page.

Locations: BL (4 MAR 39); Kent (dj).

A 1.2.b
First English edition, second printing: London: Hamish Hamilton, [March 1939].

'First cheap edition' May 1940: reprinted September 1940, January 1947, February 1948, May 1949, April 1950, November 1951. Also reprinted by Thriller Book Club (London, 1940).

A 1.3
Third edition: New York: Avon, [1942].

Murder Mystery Monthly #7. 25¢. Wrappers.

A 1.4
Fourth edition: New York: Avon, [1943].

New Avon Library #38. 25¢. Wrappers. Noted with variant ads on inside back wrapper: (a) listing of titles 3–58; (b) listing of titles 14–73. 3 printings, 1943–1945.

A 1.5.a
Fifth edition, first printing: Raymond Chandler's Mystery Omnibus. Cleveland and New York: World, [1944].

See AA 1. Reprinted 1945 (A 1.5.b).

THE BIG SLEEP

RAYMOND CHANDLER

Not since Dashiell Hammett first appeared has there been a murder mystery story with the power, pace, and terrifying atmosphere of this one. And like Hammett's this is more than a "murder mystery": it is a novel of crime and character, written with uncommon skill and in a tight, tense style which is irresistible.

The centre of the plot is a family: an old, paralyzed ex-soldier, who made a fortune in oil; his two beautiful daughters—one a gambler, the other a degenerate; and a strangely missing son-in-law. Around such a family, with all its money, its vices, and its hidden scandals, it was inevitable that there should cluster blackmailers, gangsters, and purveyors of forbidden thrills. There are violence and shameful things in the family's history, but the detective—shrewd, strong, incorruptible, the healthy force amid the shadows and the whispers—who started out to break a blackmail case and ended up to his neck in a series of mysterious murders, clears the atmosphere and leaves the reader content that justice, though of an unexpected sort, will after all be done.

We recommend this novel with enthusiasm. In our opinion it will repeat the success of *The Postman Always Rings Twice*.

Selected Thrillers, Spring 1939

THE HAND OF KORNELIUS VOYT
by OLIVER ONIONS

Sober and convincing, yet mystifying and macabre, this extraordinary novel displays its author's brilliant ability in its highest degree. 7s 6d net

LAM TO THE SLAUGHTER
by A. A. FAIR

The greatest find amongst detective stories in the past decade. This is a mystery-sensation novel with a difference. It has wit, punch, toughness and ingenuity. 7s 6d net

THE BIG SLEEP
by RAYMOND CHANDLER

A murder mystery story with power, pace, and terrifying atmosphere a novel of crime and character, written with uncommon skill and in a tense style which is irresistible. 7s 6d net

HAMISH HAMILTON
90 Great Russell Street, London, WC1

Dust jacket for A1.2.a

A 1.5.c
Fifth edition, third printing: The Big Sleep. Cleveland & New York: World, [1946].

Copyright page: 'A FORUM BOOK MOTION PICTURE EDITION | *First Printing June 1946*'.

A 1.6
Sixth edition: New York: Editions for the Armed Services, [1945].

#751. Wrappers.

A 1.7
Seventh edition: Stockholm & London: Continental, 1947.

Zephyr #148. Wrappers. Not seen.

A 1.8
Eighth edition: Harmondsworth: Penguin/in association with Hamish Hamilton, [1948].

#652. 1/6. Wrappers. Reprinted 1949, 1950, 1951, 1952, 1953, 1955, 1959, 1962, 1964, 1966, 1967, 1971, 1973, 1974, 1976.

A 1.9
Ninth edition: New York: Pocket, [1950].

#696. 25¢. Wrappers. 6 printings, 1950–1967.

A 1.10
Tenth edition: The Raymond Chandler Omnibus. London: Hamish Hamilton, [1953].

15s. See AA 6.

A 1.11
Eleventh edition: A Treasury of Great Mysteries. Edited by Howard Haycraft and John Beecroft. Vol. 2. New York: Simon & Schuster, [1957].

$5.95.

A 1.12
Twelfth edition: The Raymond Chandler Omnibus. Edited by Lawrence Clark Powell. New York: Knopf, 1964.

$5.95. See AA 10.

A 1.13
Thirteenth edition: London: Hamish Hamilton, [1967].

21s. A Fingerprint Book.

A 1.14
Fourteenth edition: New York: Knopf, [1969].

Published by the Mystery Guild as part of 10-volume Hall of Fame Mystery Set. 9 printings, 1969–1976.

A 1.15.a
Fifteenth edition, Ballantine printings: New York: Ballantine, [1971].

#02201•7•095. 95¢. Wrappers. 7 printings, 1971–1975. Possible Canadian printing.

A 1.15.b
Fifteenth edition, Vintage printing: New York: Vintage, [1976].

#V-136. $1.95. Wrappers.

A 1.16
Sixteenth edition: Bath: Lythway Press, [1976].

Large-type edition.

Note

Screenplay: Film Scripts One. Edited by George P. Garrett, O. B. Hardison, Jr., and Jane R. Gelfman (New York: Appleton-Century-Crofts, [1971]), pp. 137–329.

Screenplay for *The Big Sleep* by William Faulkner, Leigh Brackett, and Jules Furthman.

A 2 FAREWELL, MY LOVELY

A 2.1.a
First edition, first printing (1940)

raymond
chandler

*Farewell,
my
Lovely*

NEW YORK · ALFRED · A · KNOPF · LONDON

1940

A 2.1.a: 7³/₈″ × 4¹⁵/₁₆″

Copyright 1940 by Raymond Chandler. All rights reserved. No part of this book may be reproduced in any form without permission in writing from the publisher, except by a reviewer who may quote brief passages in a review to be printed in a magazine or newspaper. Manufactured in the United States of America. Published simultaneously in Canada by The Ryerson Press.

FIRST EDITION

[i–viii] [1–3] 4–275 [276–280]

[1–18]⁸

Contents: p. i: blank; p. ii: 'ALSO BY RAYMOND CHANDLER [blurb for *The Big Sleep*]'; p. iii: half title; p. iv: blank; p. v: title page; p. vi: copyright page; p. vii: disclaimer; p. viii: blank; p. 1: half title; p. 2: blank; pp. 3–275: text; p. 276: blank; p. 277: 'A NOTE ON THE TYPE'; pp. 278–280: blank.

Typography and paper: 5³/₄″ (5⁷/₈″) × 3⁵/₈″; 34 lines per page. Running heads: rectos and versos, *'farewell, my lovely'.* Wove paper.

Binding: Medium reddish orange (#37) V cloth (smooth); front, back, and spine stamped in deep blue (#179). Front: '[within single-rule frame and oval] raymond | chandler | [script] Farewell, | my | Lovely'. Spine: '[2 lines in script] Raymond | Chandler | [3 lines within single-rule frame and oval] FAREWELL, | MY | LOVELY | [line of loops] | *Alfred A Knopf* | [line of dots]'. Back: '[lower right: borzoi device] *BORZOI*'. White endpapers. All edges trimmed. Top edge stained dark blue.

Dust jacket: Front and spine printed against reddish brown background. Front: '[blue clouds and converging light blue lines] | [beige outlined in dark reddish brown] FARE [reddish brown outlined in dark reddish brown and beige] WELL, | [off-white] | *my Lovely* | [vertical signature of artist in red] | [blue] *By Raymond Chandler* | [reddish brown] AUTHOR OF "THE BIG SLEEP" '. Spine: '[brown] | *Raymond* | *Chandler* | [beige] FAREWELL, | *my Lovely* | [continuation of light blue lines] | [black Borzoi Books seal in box] | [reddish brown] ALFRED•A• | KNOPF'. Back: '[white against reddish brown box] MYSTERY AND ADVENTURE [titles in reddish brown and blue against white]'. Front flap: blurb. Back flap: note on Chandler and ad for *TBS*.

Publication: 7,500 copies of the first printing. Published 1 October 1940. $2.00. Copyright 1 October 1940. Copyright #A144970.

Printing: Composed, printed, and bound by H. Wolff, New York City.

Locations: Kent (dj); Lilly (dj).

Review copy

First-printing sheets bound in wrappers made from dust jacket. Yellow promotional slip laid in.

Location: Kent.

A 2.1.b
First edition, second printing: New York: Knopf, [1945].

Copyright page: 'First issued as a BLACK WIDOW THRILLER May 1945'.

$2.00.

$2.00 net

FAREWELL, my Lovely

• THERE is a hint of cruelty at the very beginning, a hint of a world in which viciousness is normal; and as the story develops, the atmosphere becomes increasingly malevolent and charged with evil. A giant who did not know his own strength, a Negro with a broken neck, a gin-drinking drab with a flair for malice, a ravishingly beautiful blonde with no morals and a husband who was rich and sadly tolerant, an Indian with the air of a clerk of a charlatan who called himself a psychic consultant, a doctor with a plug ugly for an assistant, a gambler and an honest cop and several crooked ones—such are the characters whom Marlowe, the private detective, meets in this tight, tense, and utterly fascinating novel of murder.

It is a shocking book—as if a thrilling one. It is difficult to imagine the reader who could put it down unfinished. In *The Big Sleep* Mr. Chandler gave notice that a new star had arrived in the field of murder mystery fiction: in this new book he proves that he is a star of the first magnitude.

FAREWELL, my Lovely

By Raymond Chandler

AUTHOR OF "THE BIG SLEEP"

"ALFRED·A· KNOPF

MYSTERY AND ADVENTURE in new BORZOI BOOKS

Farewell, my Lovely by Raymond Chandler

Shocks and thrills aplenty lie ahead in this fast, close-knit, and utterly hard-boiled story of murder, extortion, and assorted rackets and depravities on the criminal fringes of Los Angeles. Readers of *The Big Sleep* know what to expect of Mr. Chandler; all others have a real experience in store. $2.00

The Glass Triangle by George Harmon Coxe

Kent Murdock, ace newspaper photographer and amateur detective, is up against the toughest problem of his career in this new case of murder by the author of *Four Frightened Women*. "This is Mr. Coxe at his best, which means that, no matter where you search, you won't find a better thriller."—*New York World-Telegram*. $2.00

Journey Into Fear by Eric Ambler

A new novel of international intrigue and murder by the author of *A Coffin for Dimitrios*. This is the enthralling story of an English engineer returning home from Turkey, with the agents of two great powers fighting to take his life and others' to defend it. In sheer story-telling, in carrying an aura of grim suspense, in exposing the secrets behind the headlines, Mr. Ambler has no equal today. $2.00

Brink to Yesterday by Manning Coles

They found him dead in his bedroom, a revolver by his side, a hole in his head. "Death by misadventure," was the coroner's verdict. But it was murder. He had been a British spy who had become a French flics, and Germany would have its revenge. . . . A fast-paced story of intrigue, danger, and adventure, by a new star on the thriller horizon. $2.00

Raymond Chandler

was born in Chicago, of an American Quaker father and an Irish Quaker mother. At an early age he went to England, had his schooling at Dulwich College, and completed his education in France and Germany. Since then he has held many professions—teacher, book-reviewer, poet, paragraph writer, magazine writer, for a Canadian infantry regiment, student pilot, accountant, and executive and pulp writer. For the past twenty years he has lived in the United States, his home being in the Southern California area which forms the background for his books. *Farewell, my Lovely* is the second of these; the first was

The Big Sleep

"In the hard-boiled tradition and it is a honey of a hard one . . . swift, vividly spoken and hard."—*New York World-Telegram and Sun*

"Something a good deal more than a whodunit, if you have any feeling for adult workmanship, don't give it the go-by."—*New Republic*

$2.00

Alfred·A·Knopf
PUBLISHER · NEW YORK

Dust jacket for A.2.1.a

A 2.2.a
First English edition, first printing (1940)

FAREWELL, MY LOVELY

by

RAYMOND CHANDLER

HAMISH HAMILTON
LONDON

A 2.2.a: 4⁵/₈″ × 7⁵/₁₆″

Copyright page: 'First published 1940 / MADE AND PRINTED IN GREAT BRITAIN BY PURNELL AND SONS, LTD., | PAULTON (SOMERSET) AND LONDON'.

[1–6] 7–320

[A] B–I K–U⁸

Contents: p. 1: half title; p. 2: *'by the same Author'*; p. 3: title page; p. 4: copyright page; p. 5: half title; p. 6: blank; pp. 7–320: text.

Typography and paper: 5¼" (5¾") × 3½"; 32 lines per page. Running heads: rectos and versos, 'FAREWELL, MY LOVELY'. Wove paper.

Binding: Yellow V cloth (smooth); front and spine stamped in red. Front: 'FAREWELL, MY LOVELY'. Spine: 'FAREWELL, | MY | LOVELY | RAYMOND | CHANDLER | HAM-ISH | HAMILTON'. White endpapers. All edges trimmed.

Dust jacket: Not seen. A dust jacket has been reported with this front: 'Farewell, | My Lovely | [hand holding revolver] | RAYMOND | CHANDLER'.

Publication: Unknown number of copies of the first printing. Published October 1940. 7/6.

Printing: See copyright page.

Locations: BL (11 OCT 40); BOD (OCT 25 1940).

A 2.2.b

Second printing: London: Hamish Hamilton, [1941].

Reprinted 1946.

A 2.3
Third edition: New York: Pocket, [1943].

#212. 25¢. Wrappers. Reprinted 1943 (4 times), 1944, 1945 (3 times), 1951.

A 2.4.a
Fourth edition, first printing: Raymond Chandler's Mystery Omnibus. Cleveland & New York: World, [1944].

See AA 1. Reprinted 1945 (A 2.4.b).

A 2.4.c
Fourth edition, third printing: Farewell, My Lovely. Cleveland & New York: World, [1944].

Copyright page: 'TOWER BOOKS EDITION | *First printing October 1944*'.

Reprinted 1945 and 1946.

A 2.5
Fifth edition: [Harmondsworth]: Penguin/in association with Hamish Hamilton, [1949].

#701. 1/6. Wrappers. Reprinted 1950, 1952, 1954, 1956, 1959, 1961, 1966, 1971, 1973, 1975 (twice).

A 2.6
Sixth edition: London: Hamish Hamilton, [1949].

7/6. Reprinted 1949, 1951, 1953, 1958, 1960.

A 2.7

Seventh edition: The Raymond Chandler Omnibus. London: Hamish Hamilton, [1953].

15s. See AA 6.

A 2.8

Eighth edition: The Raymond Chandler Omnibus. Edited by Lawrence Clark Powell. New York: Knopf, 1964.

$5.95. See AA 10.

A 2.9

Ninth edition: New York: Pocket, [1964].

#4002. 45¢. Wrappers.

A 2.10

Tenth edition: Fifty Years. Edited by Clifton Fadiman. New York: Knopf, 1964.

A 2.11

Eleventh edition: Farewell, My Lovely & The Lady in the Lake. New York: Modern Library, [1967].

Copyright page: 'FIRST MODERN LIBRARY EDITION, February, 1967'.

#377. $2.45.

A 2.12

Twelfth edition: New York: Pocket, [1968].

#55058. 60¢. Wrappers.

A 2.13

Thirteenth edition: London: Hamish Hamilton, [1968].

25s. A Fingerprint Book. Reprinted 1971, 1976.

A 2.14.a

Fourteenth edition, Ballantine printings: New York: Ballantine, [1971].

#22202•4•095. 95¢. Wrappers. 7 printings, 1971–1975. Possible Canadian printing.

A 2.14.b

Fourteenth edition, Vintage printing: New York: Vintage, [1976].

#V-138. $1.95. Wrappers.

A 3 THE HIGH WINDOW

A 3.1.a
First edition, first printing (1942)

A 3.1.a: 7¹/₂″ × 5¹/₈″

Copyright 1942 by Raymond Chandler
All rights reserved. No part of this book may be reproduced in any form without permission in writing from the publisher, except by a reviewer who may quote brief passages in a review to be printed in a magazine or newspaper. Manufactured in the United States of America. Published simultaneously in Canada by The Ryerson Press
FIRST EDITION

[i–x] [1–2] 3–240 [241–246]

[1–16]⁸

Contents: pp. i–ii: blank; p. iii: 'the high window [20-line blurb]'; p. iv: 'ALSO BY RAYMOND CHANDLER [quotes from reviews of *TBS* and *FML*]'; p. v: half title; p. vi: blank; p. vii: title page: p. viii: copyright page; p. ix: disclaimer; p. x: blank; p. 1: half title; p. 2: blank; pp. 3–240: text; p. 241: blank; p. 242: 'A NOTE ON THE TYPE'; pp. 243–246: blank.

Typography and paper: 5¹/₄″ (5⁹/₁₆″) × 3⁵/₈″; 32 lines per page. Running heads: rectos and versos, 'the high window'. Wove paper.

Binding: Light grayish brown (#60) V cloth (smooth); front, back, and spine stamped in dark purplish red (#259). Front: '[within single-rule frame and oval] raymond | chandler | [script] The High | Window'. Spine: '[2 lines in script] Raymond | Chandler | [3 lines within single-rule frame and oval] THE | HIGH | WINDOW | [line of loops] | *Alfred A Knopf*'. Back: '[lower right: borzoi device] | *BORZOI*'. White endpapers. Top edge trimmed.

Dust jacket: Front and spine printed against blue background. Front: '[window, clouds, and falling man] [white] the [yellow] high [white] window | [mountains, scale, invoice, pistol, magnifying glass, and gold coins in white, yellow, and blue] | [white] RAYMOND CHANDLER | AUTHOR OF [yellow] "THE BIG SLEEP" '. Spine: '[white] RAYMOND | CHANDLER | [man falling from window] | [white] the [yellow] high | [white] window | [yellow Borzoi Books seal in box] | [white] ALFRED•A• | KNOPF'. Back: '[blue] A MESSAGE | *to the reader of* | *this book from* | RAYMOND | CHAN-DLER | [photo of Chandler and 20-line statement about War Bonds]'. Front flap: blurb. Back flap: quotes from reviews of *TBS* and *FML*.

Publication: 6,500 copies of the first printing. Published 17 August 1942. $2.00. Copyright 17 August 1942. Copyright #A16696.

Printing: Composed, printed, and bound by H. Wolff, New York City.

Locations: Kent (dj); LC (JUL-6 1942, rebound); Lilly (dj).

A 3.1.b
First edition, second printing: New York: Grosset & Dunlap, 1943.

Not seen.

A 3.1.c
First edition, third printing: New York: Knopf, [1945].

Copyright page: 'First issued as a BLACK WIDOW THRILLER May 1945'.

$2.00.

the high window

It started with some business about a rare coin. Everybody knew who had stolen it, but nobody was anxious to do anything about it.

Marlowe couldn't understand why the old lady had hired him, she didn't seem to like detectives and she didn't want to tell him much. So he started to think about her, and then about the pale, fragile, frightened little girl who was her secretary, and then about her son—which led him to the gambler, and then to the gambler's luscious and lustful wife, and then to the elegant blackmailer.

And so the case became a study of character, for even when murder was done, even after the second murder, character was the root of everything. Because he understood that, Marlowe went step by step to a solution of the case. Sardonic, quietly cynical, cold and merciless when he has to be, but gruffly compassionate toward the victims of evil, Marlowe steps out of these unfolding pages as one of the great detectives of modern murder-mystery fiction.

No part of the book has appeared in any magazine or periodical in the United States.

Other Books by
RAYMOND CHANDLER

The Big Sleep

"So definitely on the superior side that even readers who ordinarily shun mysteries will find this novel well worth respecting. It has the shock appeal and keen manner of books by Dashiell Hammett and James Cain, and the story races through to a surprise climax that lifts some sort of high in sheer ingenuity."
—*Pittsburgh Post-Gazette*

"I hope it may be the first of a long series, for this fellow knows how to write. There is action in his work, and there is passion, bad atmosphere and character. And what more do you want for your two books?"
—*Cleveland Plain Dealer*

Farewell, My Lovely

"All set to sneer kettels, at another tough item, balled as 'a shocking book—and a thrilling one,' this department soon succumbed to what strikes us as the real thing in wickedness—and the best hard-boiled mystery in ages.... Grade A."
—Will Cuppy, *New York Herald Tribune 'Books'*

"A thrilling book, a story of easy people and incredibly brutal people. Chandler tells it with a raw richness of simple seldom seen in a detective yarn. You won't be able to put it down."
—*San Francisco Call-Bulletin*

A MESSAGE
to the reader of this book from
RAYMOND CHANDLER

"I am one of those who believe that in a time of great national crisis a government of the people, for the people, should take what it needs from the people. So far our government, in the matter of War Bonds and Stamps, is not taking; it is asking—and rather gently and politely at that. And it is not even asking that people give, but that they spend something which shall be returned to them with interest added.

"As usual in such situations I suppose the quick and the generous people are doing more than their share, that the hard and selfish are doing less. Between these two extremes lies the great mass of loyal Americans who have hearts and understanding, but whose hearts sometimes have to be moved for them, whose understanding sometimes needs a vision. Such a vision is all any writer, important or unimportant, has any right to offer.

"However great and rich a country may be, the cost of this war, spent, planned and projected, is like a space of water upon which by a miracle men must walk. It is a terrible place, lonely and enormous, dark with clouds, and the air above it is shaken with thunder. Only the faith of the little people can cross it. But Americans have never been too cynical to have a share in a miracle. In buying our country's War Bonds and Stamps it seems to me we are doing just that."

ALFRED · A · KNOPF   PUBLISHER · N · Y

RAYMOND CHANDLER

the high window

RAYMOND CHANDLER

the high window

BORZOI BOOKS

ALFRED·A·KNOPF

RAYMOND CHANDLER
AUTHOR OF "THE BIG SLEEP"

Dust jacket for A.3.1.a

A 3.1.d

First edition, fourth printing: Cleveland & New York: World, [1945].

Copyright page: 'TOWER BOOKS EDITION | *First Printing August 1945*'.

Reprinted 1946 with dust-jacket title, *The Brasher Dubloon.*

A 3.2
First English edition, first printing (1943)

THE
HIGH WINDOW

by
Raymond Chandler

Hamish Hamilton
LONDON

A 3.2: 4⁵/₈″ × 7⁵/₁₆″

Copyright page: 'First published 1943 | PRINTED IN GREAT BRITAIN | BY WEST-ERN PRINTING SERVICES LTD., BRISTOL'.

[1–4] 5–236 [237–240]

[A] B–I K–P⁸

Contents: p. 1: half title; p. 2: *'by the same author';* p. 3: title page; p. 4: copyright page; pp. 5–236: text; pp. 237–240: endpapers. (The Hamish Hamilton file copy and the Bodleian copy have pp. 237–240 as the free and pastedown rear endpapers; the British Library copy has pp. 237–240 excised and binder's endpapers.)

Typography and paper: 5³/₄" (6") × 3⁵/₈"; 35 lines per page. Running heads: rectos and versos, 'THE HIGH WINDOW'. Wove paper.

Binding: Reddish orange V cloth (smooth). Spine goldstamped: 'THE | HIGH | WIN-DOW | RAYMOND | CHANDLER | [hh device] | HAMISH | HAMILTON'. White end-papers. All edges trimmed.

Dust jacket: Front printed against yellow background, showing blonde in blue dress stepping on a pistol: '[white against red panel] THE HIGH WINDOW | [blue] RAY-MOND CHANDLER | AUTHOR OF "THE BIG SLEEP"'. Spine printed against red background: '[yellow] THE | HIGH | WINDOW | [star] | [white] RAYMOND | CHAN-DLER | [yellow woman with pistol] | [white] HAMISH | HAMILTON'. Back printed in blue against white background: 'LATEST | FICTION'. Front flap: ad for *THW* printed in blue against white background. Back flap blank.

Publication: Unknown number of copies of the first printing. Published February 1943. 8s.

Printing: See copyright page.

Locations: BL (16 FEB 43); BOD (FEB 22 1943); Hamish Hamilton (dj).

A 3.3
Third edition: New York: Pocket, 1945.

25¢. Wrappers. Not seen. 5 printings, 1945–1965.

A 3.4
Fourth edition: London & Stockholm: Continental, 1948.

Zephyr. Wrappers. Not seen.

A 3.5
Fifth edition: [Harmondsworth]: Penguin/in association with Hamish Hamilton, [1951].

#851. 1/6. Wrappers. Reprinted 1952, 1954, 1956, 1959, 1961, 1963, 1967, 1971, 1973, 1976, 1977.

A 3.6
Sixth edition: The Raymond Chandler Omnibus. London: Hamish Hamilton, [1953].

15s. See AA 6.

A 3.7
Seventh edition: The Raymond Chandler Omnibus. Edited by Lawrence Clark Powell. New York: Knopf, 1964.

$5.95. See AA 10.

A 3.8
Ninth edition. London: Hamish Hamilton, [1967].

21s. A Fingerprint Book. Reprinted 1970, 1973.

A 3.9.a
Eighth edition, Pocket printing. New York: Pocket, [1969].

#55062. 60¢. Wrappers.

A 3.9.b
Eighth edition, Vintage printing. New York: Vintage, [1976].

Copyright page: 'FIRST VINTAGE BOOKS EDITION, September 1976'.

#V-141. $1.95. Wrappers.

A 4 THE LADY IN THE LAKE

A 4.1.a
First edition, first printing (1943)

A 4.1.a: 7⁷/₁₆″ × 5¹/₄″

> *Copyright 1943 by Raymond Chandler*
> *All rights reserved. No part of this book may be reproduced in any form without permission in writing from the publisher, except by a reviewer who may quote brief passages in a review to be printed in a magazine or newspaper. Manufactured in the United States of America. Published simultaneously in Canada by The Ryerson Press.*
> **FIRST EDITION**
>
> This book has been produced in full compliance with all government regulations for the conservation of paper, metal, and other essential materials.

[i–vi] [1–2] 3–216 [217–218]

[1–14]^8

Contents: p. i: 'the lady in the lake [16-line blurb]'; p. ii: 'ALSO BY RAYMOND CHANDLER [quotes from reviews of *TBS, FML,* and *THW*]'; p. iii: half title; p. iv: blank; p. v: title page; p. vi: copyright page; p. 1: half title; p. 2: blank; pp. 3–216: text; p. 217: blank; p. 218: 'A NOTE ON THE TYPE'.

Typography and paper: 5^9/$_{16}$″ (5^3/$_4$″) × 3^3/$_4$″; 36 lines per page. Running heads: rectos and versos, *'the lady in the lake'*. Wove paper.

Binding: Medium yellowish green (#136) V cloth (smooth); front, back, and spine stamped in vivid dark green (#147). Front: '[within single-rule frame and oval] raymond | chandler | [script] The Lady | in the | Lake'. Spine: '[2 lines in script] Raymond | Chandler | [3 lines within single-rule frame and oval] | THE LADY | IN THE | LAKE | [line of loops] | Alfred A Knopf'. Back: '[lower right: borzoi device] BORZOI'. White endpapers. Top and bottom edges trimmed.

Dust jacket: Front and spine printed in light purple against black. Front: 'The Lady | IN THE Lake | [white house on purple mountain; black figures in foreground] | RAY-MOND CHANDLER | A PHILIP MARLOWE MYSTERY'. Spine: 'The | Lady | in the | Lake | [lightning and tree] | RAYMOND | CHANDLER | [Borzoi Books seal in box] | ALFRED•A• | KNOPF'. Back: Chandler's War Bonds message in black against white; see *THW*. Front flap: blurb. Back flap: quotes from ads for *TBS, FML,* and *THW*.

Publication: 6,000 copies of the first printing. Published 1 November 1943. $2.00. Copyright 1 November 1943. Copyright #A176547.

Printing: Composed, printed, and bound by H. Wolff, New York City.

Locations: Kent (dj); LC (OCT 11 1943, rebound); Lilly (dj).

A 4.1.b
First edition, second printing: New York: Knopf, 1943.

Copyright page: *'First and Second Printings before Publication'.*

A 4.1.c
First edition, third printing: New York: Knopf, 1944.

Not seen.

A 4.1.d
First edition, fourth printing: New York: Grosset & Dunlap, [1943].

Binding variants.

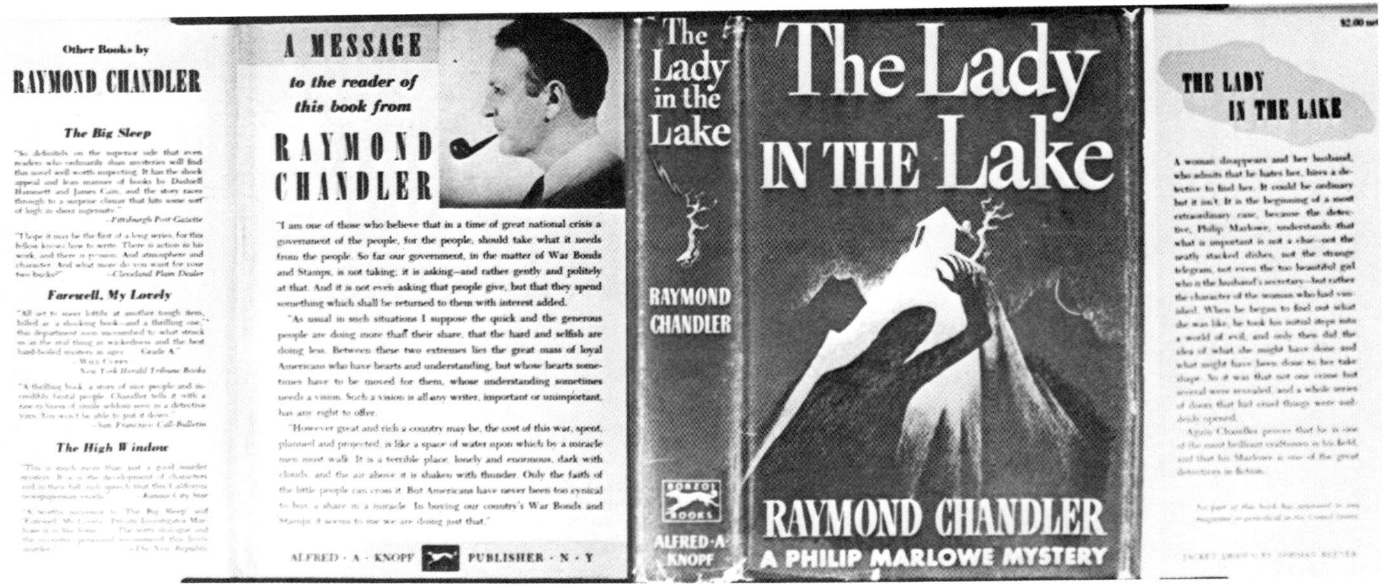

Dust jacket for A 4.1.a

A 4.1.e
First edition, fifth printing: New York: Knopf, [1945].

Copyright page: '*First issued as a BLACK WIDOW THRILLER May 1945*'.

Reprinted August 1945.

A 4.2.a
First English edition, first printing (1944)

THE LADY
IN THE LAKE

by
Raymond Chandler

Hamish Hamilton
LONDON

A 4.2.a: 7³/₁₆″ × 4³/₄″

Copyright page: 'First published 1944 | PRINTED IN GREAT BRITAIN | BY WEST-ERN PRINTING SERVICES, LTD., BRISTOL'.

[1–4] 5–212

[A] B–F^{16} G^{10}

Contents: p. 1: half title; p. 2: *'By the same Author';* p. 3: title page; p. 4: copyright page; pp. 5–212: text.

Typography and paper: 5^3/$_4$" (5^7/$_8$") × 3^5/$_8$"; 38 lines per page. Running heads: rectos and versos, 'THE LADY IN THE LAKE'. Wove paper.

Binding: Strong orange yellow (#68) V cloth (smooth). Spine stamped in strong reddish orange (#35): 'THE | LADY | IN THE | LAKE | RAYMOND | CHANDLER | [HH device] | HAMISH | HAMILTON'. White endpapers. All edges trimmed.

Dust jacket: Not seen.

Publication: Unknown number of copies of the first printing. Published October 1944. 8/6.

Printing: See copyright page.

Locations: BL (13 OCT 44); BOD (NOV 6 1944); Kent.

A 4.2.b
First English edition, second printing: London: Hamish Hamilton, [1944].

Reprinted 1945 (twice), 1947, 1949.

A 4.3
Third edition: New York: Editions for the Armed Services, [1945].

#838. Wrappers.

A 4.4
Fourth edition: New York: Pocket, [1946].

#389. 25¢. Wrappers. 5 printings, 1946–1954.

A 4.5
Fifth edition: Stockholm & London: Continental, [1948?].

Zephyr #162. Wrappers.

A 4.6
Sixth edition: [Harmondsworth]: Penguin/in association with Hamish Hamilton, [1952].

#867. 2s. Wrappers. Reprinted 1954, 1955, 1959, 1961, 1966, 1971, 1973, 1975, 1976.

A 4.7
Seventh edition: The Raymond Chandler Omnibus. London: Hamish Hamilton, [1953].

15s. See AA 6.

A 4.8
Eighth edition: New York: Pocket, [1959].

#C-344. 35¢. Wrappers. Reprinted 1966.

A 4.9
Ninth edition: Three Times Three. Edited by Howard Haycraft and John Beecroft. Garden City: Doubleday, [1964], pp. 11–188.

Also distributed by one of the Doubleday book clubs.

A 4.10
Tenth edition: The Raymond Chandler Omnibus. Edited by Lawrence Clark Powell. New York: Knopf, 1964.

$5.95. See AA 10.

A 4.11
Eleventh edition: Farewell My Lovely & The Lady in the Lake. New York: Modern Library, [1967].

Copyright page: 'FIRST MODERN LIBRARY EDITION, February, 1967'.

#377. $2.45.

A 4.12
Twelfth edition: London: Hamish Hamilton, [1969].

25s. A Fingerprint Book. Reprinted 1972, 1974.

A 4.13.a
Thirteenth edition, Ballantine printing: New York: Ballantine, [1971].

#02204•1•095. 95¢. Wrappers.

A 4.13.b
Thirteenth edition, Vintage printing: New York: Vintage, [1976].

#V-145. $1.95. Wrappers.

A 4.14
Fourteenth edition: New York & London: Garland, 1976.

Fifty Classics of Crime Fiction series, ed. Jacques Barzun and Wendell H. Taylor.

A 5 FIVE MURDERERS

A 5.1
First edition, first printing (1944)

A 5.1: 7⁹/₁₆″ × 5¹/₄″

[9–10] 11–166 [167–168]

Perfect binding.

Contents: p. 9: title; p. 10: 'For | JOSEPH THOMPSON SHAW | with affection and respect, and in memory of | the time when we were trying to get murder | away from the upper classes, the week-end house | party and the vicar's rose-garden, and back | to the people who are really good at it.'; pp. 11–166: text; p. 167: ad for *The Embezzler!;* p. 168: ad for *Avon Murder Mystery Monthly.*

   5 stories: "Goldfish," "Spanish Blood," "Blackmailers Don't Shoot," "Guns at Cyrano's," "Nevada Gas." All first book appearances. See C 40, C 44–C 46, C 49.

Typography and paper: 6^{11}/$_{16}$″ (7″) × 4^{7}/$_{16}$″; 48 lines per page. Running heads: rectos, story titles; versos, 'FIVE MURDERERS'. Wove paper.

Binding: Printed paper wrappers. Front: '[against dark gray olive green (#128) background] [white] *By the author of* "THE BIG SLEEP" | [left: 2 brilliant yellow (#83) boxes] [top box: black and white skull] [lower box: black] MURDER | MYSTERY | MONTHLY | [right: white shaded in vivid red orange (#34)] 5 | [center] MURDERERS | [5 heads] | [vivid light blue green (#162)] RAYMOND | CHANDLER'. Spine: '[vertical] [white against light orange (#52) panel] RAYMOND CHANDLER [white shaded in black against brilliant yellow green (#116) panel] 5 *MURDERERS* | [horizontal] [black rule] [2 brilliant yellow boxes] [top box: black and white skull] [lower box: black] MURDER | MYSTERY | MONTHLY | [black rule] [black within white circle against brilliant yellow green panel] 19'. Back: ads for *The Embezzler!* and *The Moon Pool!* in black against white and brilliant yellow. Inside front: statement by Joseph T. Shaw and quote from *Coronet.* Inside back: ad for *Avon Murder Mystery Monthly.* All edges trimmed.

Publication: Unknown number of copies of the first printing. Published 3 February 1944. 25¢. Copyright 3 February 1944. Copyright #AA461138.

Printing: Composed, printed, and bound by J. W. Clement, Buffalo, N.Y.

Locations: Kent; Harvard.

A 5.2
Second edition: New York: Avon, [1945].

New Avon Library, #63. 25¢. Wrappers. 3 printings noted: (a) publisher's address on title page is 432 Fourth Ave.; last ad on inside back wrapper is for title 63; (b) publisher's address on title page is 119 W. 57th St.; last ad on inside back wrapper is for title 70; (c) publisher's address on title page is 119 W. 57th St.; last ad on inside back wrapper is for title 77.

Front wrapper of A 5.1

A 6 FIVE SINISTER CHARACTERS

A 6.1
First edition, first printing (1945)

FIVE SINISTER CHARACTERS

By

RAYMOND CHANDLER

Author of "The Big Sleep"

MURDER MYSTERY MONTHLY

No. 28

AVON BOOK COMPANY
JO MEYERS   •   **E. B. WILLIAMS**
432 FOURTH AVENUE, NEW YORK 16, N.Y.

Published by special arrangement with
Mr. Raymond Chandler

A 6.1: 7⁵/₈″ × 5¹/₄″

CONTENTS

Trouble Is My Business, *Copyright, August, 1939, by Dime Detective.* Pearls Are a Nuisance, *Copyright, April, 1939, by Dime Detective.* I'll Be Waiting, *Copyright, October 14, 1939, by Saturday Evening Post.* The King in Yellow, *Copyright, March, 1938, by Dime Detective.* Red Wind, *Copyright, January, 1938, by Dime Detective.*
Five Sinister Characters, *Copyright, 1945, by Avon Book Company.* Printed in U.S.A.

[9–11] 12–168

Perfect binding.

Contents: p. 9: title page; p. 10: contents and copyrights; pp. 11–168: text.
5 *stories:* "Trouble Is My Business," "Pearls Are a Nuisance," "I'll Be Waiting," "The King in Yellow," "Red Wind." All first book appearances. See C 55, C 56, C 59–C 61.

Typography and paper: $7^1/_{16}''$ ($7^3/_{16}''$) × $4^7/_{16}''$; 46 lines per page. No running heads. Wove paper.

Binding: Printed paper wrappers. Front: '[black] By the author of "THE BIG SLEEP" | [left: 2 brilliant yellow (#83) boxes] [top box: black and white skull] [lower box: black] MURDER | MYSTERY | MONTHLY | [right: vivid red orange (#34) outlined in white] FIVE | SINISTER | CHARACTERS | [black] BY | RAYMOND CHANDLER | [below: head of woman with 4 smaller heads]'. Spine: '[vertical] [black against strong yellow green (#117) panel] RAYMOND CHANDLER [black against vivid red orange panel] 5 SINISTER CHARACTERS | [horizontal] [2 brilliant yellow boxes] [top box: black and white skull] [lower box: black] MURDER | MYSTERY | MONTHLY [in black against vivid red orange circle] 28'. Back: '[black against white and light yellow green (#119)] *Place Your Order Now!* [ads for *The Face in the Abyss!* and *The Black Angel*]'. Inside front: '*You Can Never Get Enough of Chandler* [blurbs for stories]'. Inside back: 'MURDER MYSTERY MONTHLY [23 titles]'. All edges trimmed.

Publication: Unknown number of copies of the first printing. Published 14 February 1934. 25¢. Copyright 14 February 1945. Copyright #478677.

Printing: Composed, printed, and bound by J. W. Clement, Buffalo, N.Y.

Locations: Kent; Lilly.

A 6.2
Second edition: New York: Avon, [1946].
New Avon Library #88. 25¢. Wrappers.

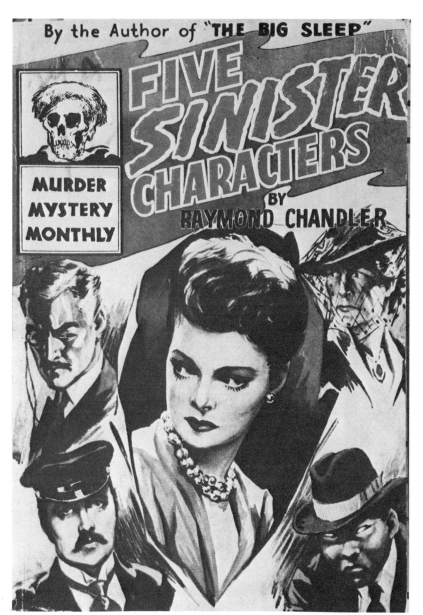

By the Author of "THE BIG SLEEP"

FIVE SINISTER CHARACTERS

BY RAYMOND CHANDLER

MURDER MYSTERY MONTHLY

Front wrapper of A 6.1

A 7 FINGER MAN

A 7.1
First edition, first printing (1947)

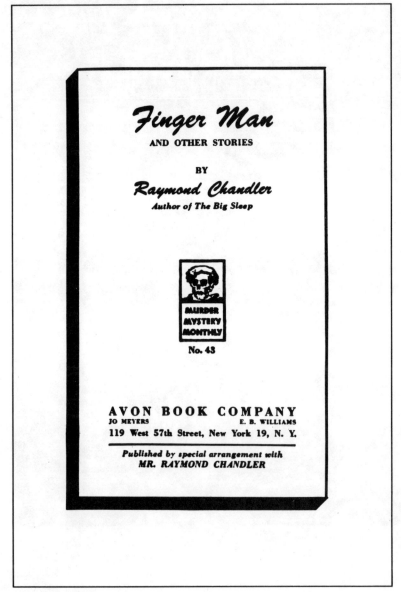

A 7.1: 7⁷/₁₆″ × 5¹/₄″

FINGER MAN
Copyright, October, 1934, by Black Mask Magazine

THE BRONZE DOOR
Copyright, November, 1939, by Street & Smith Publications

SMART-ALECK KILL
Copyright, June, 1934, by Black Mask Magazine

THE SIMPLE ART OF MURDER
Copyright, 1944, by the Atlantic Monthly Company

FINGER MAN AND OTHER STORIES
Copyright, 1946, by Avon Book Company

Printed in U. S. A.

[7–10] 11–122 [123–126]

Perfect binding.

Contents: p. 7: title; p. 8: copyright; p. 9: 'CONTENTS'; p. 10: half title; pp. 11–122: text; p. 123: ad for *TBS, 5M, 5SC;* p. 124: ad for *Rex Stout's Mystery Magazine;* p. 125: ad for *Avon Short Story Monthly* (last title is #34); p. 126: ad for *New Avon Library* (last title is #97).

3 stories: "Finger Man," "The Bronze Door," and "Smart-Aleck Kill"; and "The Simple Art of Murder" (revised version). All first book appearances except "The Simple Art of Murder." See B 4, C 41, C 42, C 62, C 64.

Typography and paper: $6^5/8''$ ($6^7/8''$) $\times$ $4^1/8''$; 43 or 42 lines per page. Running heads: rectos, story titles; versos, 'RAYMOND CHANDLER'. Wove paper.

Binding: Printed paper wrappers. Front: '[vivid orange red (#34) borders at top and sides] [dark purplish red (#259) against gray purplish pink (#253) panel] RAYMOND CHANDLER | [white script against black] The [white with black fingerprint swirls] Finger | Man | [white] AND OTHER STORIES | [left: 2 brilliant yellow (#83) boxes] [top box: black and white skull] [lower box: black] MURDER | MYSTERY | MONTHLY | [below: illustration of woman and 2 men against roulette wheel, signed "Loren Gelb"]'. Spine: '[vertical] [dark purplish red against gray purplish pink panel] RAYMOND CHANDLER [white against black panel] [script] The Finger Man | [below] AND OTHER STORIES | [horizontal] [2 brilliant yellow boxes] [top box: black and white skull] [lower box: black] MURDER | MYSTERY | MONTHLY | [below: black within circle] 43'. Back: ads for *Love's Lovely Counterfeit* and *Borrowed Crime* in black against white and medium pink (#5). Inside front: blurb. Inside back: ad for *Murder Mystery Monthly* (last title is *Borrowed Crime*).

Publication: Unknown number of copies of the first printing. Published 15 April 1947. 25¢. Copyright 22 May 1947. Copyright #AA52889. Although the copyright page stipulates 1946, *Finger Man* was published in 1947; it was listed in the 13 December 1947 issue of *Publishers Weekly*.

Printing: Composed, printed, and bound by J. W. Clement, Buffalo, N.Y.

Location: Kent.

Front wrapper of A7.1

A 7.2
Second edition: New York: Avon, [1950].

New Avon Library #219. 25¢. Wrappers.

A 7.3
Third edition: London: Harborough, [1960].

Contents: "Introduction," "Pearls Are a Nuisance," "Finger Man," "The King in Yellow," "The Simple Art of Murder."

Ace H 309. 2/6.

A 8 THE LITTLE SISTER

A 8.1.a
First edition, first printing (1949)

The Little Sister

BY
RAYMOND CHANDLER

HAMISH HAMILTON
LONDON

A 8.1.a: 7¹/₄″ × 4³/₄″

Copyright page: 'First published in Great Britain, 1949 | by Hamish Hamilton, Ltd | MADE AND PRINTED IN GREAT BRITAIN BY | EBENEZER BAYLIS AND SON, LTD., THE | TRINITY PRESS, WORCESTER, AND LONDON'.

[1–4] 5–256

[A] B–I K–P R⁸

Contents: p. 1: half title; p. 2: *'By the same Author'*; p. 3: title page; p. 4: copyright page; pp. 5–256: text.

Typography and paper: $5^{15}/_{16}''$ ($6^1/_8''$) × $3^5/_8''$; 36 lines per page. No running heads. Wove paper.

Binding: Strong red (#12) V cloth (smooth). Spine goldstamped: 'THE | LITTLE | SISTER | [short thick and thin rules] | *RAYMOND* | *CHANDLER* | [HH device]'. White endpapers. All edges trimmed.

Dust jacket: Front: '[white] *The Little Sister* | [blue] *RAYMOND CHANDLER* | [woman in brown suit entering Marlowe's office, signed "CWB"]'. Spine: '[white] *The* | *Little* | *Sister* | [blue] *RAYMOND* | *CHANDLER* | [continuation of front illustration, showing man's head] | [blue] *HAMISH* | *HAMILTON*'. Back: '[black against white] AN AD-VANCE OPINION | by J. B. PRIESTLEY'. Front flap: blurb and quotes from critics. Back flap: quotes from reviews of *TLITL, THW, FML, TBS*.

Publication: Unknown number of copies of the first printing. Published 24 June 1949. 8/6. Copyright 24 June 1949. Copyright #A1-2352.

Printing: See copyright page.

Locations: BL (24 JUN 49); Kent (dj).

A8.1.b
First edition, second printing: London: Hamish Hamilton, [December 1949].

Not seen.

A8.1.c
First edition, third printing: London: Hamish Hamilton, [1950].

On copyright page: '. . . Issued by | STAR EDITIONS Ltd. | London | for sale on the Continent | of Europe only . . . . '

Dust jacket over printed wrappers.

A8.1.d
First edition, fourth printing: London: Hamish Hamilton, [1969].

25s. A Fingerprint Book. Reprinted 1971, 1976.

Other books by
RAYMOND CHANDLER

THE LADY IN THE LAKE
'It is most efficiently written: the story travels at exhilarating speed. It is a brilliant whodunit.'
—Desmond MacCarthy, *Sunday Times*

THE HIGH WINDOW
'Very tough, very tense, enormously lively.' —*Observer*

FAREWELL, MY LOVELY
'The dialogue crackles, the killer kills, the action careers a great deal of ground and hard knocks at terrific speed.' —*Spectator*

THE BIG SLEEP
'A book to be read at a sitting.' —*Sunday Times*

AN ADVANCE OPINION
by J. B. PRIESTLEY
OF

THE LITTLE SISTER

Do you ever read Raymond Chandler? I have just devoured a proof of his last story. He fascinates me, chiefly, I think, because he offers me the unusual and pleasing spectacle of a man trying to turn a cheap, popular formula into something much better. He does it, too. He accepts the familiar pattern of the contemporary thriller (American in origin but now largely and badly imitated here, where it does not really belong), the world of corpses, whisky for breakfast and luscious nymphomaniacs, but illuminates it with a genuine if sour wit and much oblique social criticism. To read him is like cutting into an over-ripe melon and discovering that it has a rare astringent flavour. He reduces the bright Californian scene to an empty despair, dead bottles and a heap of cigarette butts under the meaningless neon lights, much more adroitly than Aldous Huxley and the rest can do; and suggests, to my mind, almost better than anybody else the failure of a life that is somehow short of a dimension, with everybody else wistfully wondering what is wrong or taking savage short cuts to nowhere.
—*NEW STATESMAN, April 9th, 1949*

HAMISH HAMILTON

The Little Sister
RAYMOND CHANDLER

The
Little
Sister

RAYMOND
CHANDLER

PHILIP M...
Investigator

HAMISH
HAMILTON

8s. 6d. net

Dust jacket for A.8.1.a

A 8.2.a
First American edition, first printing (1949)

the little sister

BY RAYMOND CHANDLER

HOUGHTON MIFFLIN COMPANY · BOSTON
THE RIVERSIDE PRESS · CAMBRIDGE
1949

A 8.2.a: 7^{15}/$_{16}$″ × 5^{1}/$_{2}$″

COPYRIGHT, 1949, BY RAYMOND CHANDLER

ALL RIGHTS RESERVED INCLUDING THE RIGHT TO
REPRODUCE THIS BOOK OR PARTS THEREOF
IN ANY FORM

Part of this book has appeared in Cosmopolitan *magazine*

The Riverside Press
CAMBRIDGE · MASSACHUSETTS
PRINTED IN THE U.S.A.

[i–vi] [1] 2–249 [250]; first page of each chapter unnumbered.

[1–16]^8

Contents: p. i: half title; p. ii: 'BY RAYMOND CHANDLER'; p. iii: title page; p. iv: copyright page; p. v: half title; p. vi: blank; pp. 1–249: text; p. 250: blank.

Typography and paper: 6^7/$_{16}$″ (6^5/$_8$″) × 4^3/$_{16}$″; 36 lines per page. No running heads. Wove paper.

Binding: Deep reddish orange (#36) or medium yellow (#87) V cloth (smooth). Front: deep blue (#179) dagger with naked woman as handle. Spine: '[deep blue] *the | little | sister* | CHANDLER | HOUGHTON | MIFFLIN | CO.' White endpapers. Top edge trimmed. The orange binding presumably preceded the yellow binding.

Dust jacket: Front and spine have illustration of cloth, fly, icepick, spectacles, dressmaker's dummy. Front: '[white script with black shadow against brown] the | Little | Sister | [yellow on red shading to black] By | RAYMOND | CHANDLER | [vertically at right in black] *ARTZYBASHEFF*'. Spine: '[white] RAYMOND | CHANDLER | [script] The | [roman] LITTLE | SISTER | [yellow] HOUGHTON | MIFFLIN'. Back: '[black against white] Raymond | Chandler | [photo of Chandler at right] *Here's Marlowe* | [25 lines from pp. 77–78]'. Front flap: blurb. Back flap: continuation of blurb.

Publication: 12,500 copies of the first printing. Published 26 September 1949. $2.50. Copyright 26 September 1949. Copyright #A 36556.

Printing: Composed by J. S. Cushing, Norwood, Mass.; printed by Berwick & Smith, Norwood, Mass.; bound by O. B. Fleming, Norwood, Mass.

Locations: Kent (orange cloth, dj); LC (SEP 14 1949, both copies orange); Lilly (orange, dj); McCarty (yellow).

Note: Abridged in *Cosmopolitan,* 126 (April 1949), 173–196. See C 75.

A 8.2.b
First American edition, second printing: Boston: Houghton Mifflin, [1949].
Not seen.

A 8.2.c
First American edition, third printing: Boston: Houghton Mifflin, [1949?].
Not seen.

A 8.3
Third edition: New York: Pocket, [1950].
#750. 25¢. Wrappers. Reprint not seen.

$2.50

The Little Sister
by Raymond Chandler

Some days he's the twogun kid from Cumide Gulch and others he's only an octoplasm with a private license. But to readers of *The Big Sleep*, *Farewell, My Lovely*, *The High Window*, and *The Lady in the Lake*, he's Philip Marlowe—Man with an "e"—the most exacting high-voltage private investigator in the business.

Raymond Chandler brings him back alive in the fifth of his tense, taut, tightly meshed novels, although at the end the "little sister," a sweet exception to a sardonic Marlowe feeling like a pup from tes eridades' calendar cramped at the bottom of the watchtocker. When the reader, too, comes up for air, he doesn't know whether he's been on a two-day roller jag, or given a stand up by the Bay City cops, or blinded by the neon-lighted dame called Hollywood.

What he does know is that Marlowe will still do the goods; that his sardonic humor is running free; that his conviction is so hard that it hurts. He is in a world where a man can talk and spit without even knowing the

continued on back flap

continued from front flap

cigarette that lives in his face; where they make their drinks in glasses tall enough to stand umbrellas in; where a girl may smell like the Taj Mahal looks by moonlight but don't let that fool you—if she has a phony Spanish accent and rich bears on the sixteenth. It didn't stop Marlowe—in the end, that is.

In *The Little Sister*, Chandler is again master of his own brand of vernacular which sets it down as if he were a densely appointed recording angel to the tough guy. Few writers have banged most superlatives and held them with a former grasp, been by its sheer expression to tow human folks. If he is the creator of Philip Marlowe, he is the corridor for the chandler of it.

Raymond Chandler is the brave man who roamed round the writer's own garden and gave it back to the people who are really good at it. Knowing its high entertainment value, he is gone up a sharp eye and a always serious displays a legitimate knowledge of human motivation, most of them indecals. In addition to his keen needle and collected shots, his fine California hand can travel to some of the finest parcel movies of the past decade. "Philip Marlowe: Private Detective"—based on his invaluable character—is a popular feature. Born abroad, he had his schooling in England, France, and Germany. Before turning writer he sampled most of the occupations of the spectator gentleman.

Jacket by Bette Steinbinder

Raymond Chandler

Here's Marlowe

"A California secret. California, the department-store state. The most of everything and the best of nothing. Here we go again. You're not human tonight, Marlowe. All right. Why would I be? I'm sitting in that office, playing with a dead fly and im pop this dowdy little item from Manhattan, Kansas, and chuck me down to a shop-worn twenty to find her brother. He sounds like a creep but she wants to find him. So with this fortune clasped to my chest, I trundle down to Bay City and the routine I go through is so tired I'm half asleep on my feet. I meet nice people—with and without ice picks in their necks. I kane, and I leave myself wide-open too. Three thin comers in and takes the twenty away from me and gives me a slam and gives it back to me because I didn't do a full day's work. So I go on. By Hambleton, retired (and how) optometrist from El Centro, and meet again the new style in nickware. And I don't tell the cops. I just took the costumer's tongue and put on an act. Why? Who am I cutting my throat for this time? A blonde with wet eyes and two more door keys? A girl from Manhattan, Kansas? I don't know. All I know is that something isn't what it seems and the old tired feet always reliable hunch tells me that if the hand is played the way it is dealt the wrong person is going to lose the pot. Is that my business? Well, what is my business? Do I know? Marlowe. Maybe I never go away that well be. Maybe we all get like this in the cold half lit world where always the wrong thing happens and never the right."

RAYMOND CHANDLER
The LITTLE SISTER

The *Little Sister*

By
RAYMOND CHANDLER

HOUGHTON MIFFLIN

Dust jacket for A8.2.a

A 8.4
Fourth edition: [Harmondsworth]: Penguin/in association with Hamish Hamilton, [1955].

#1096. 2/6. Wrappers. Reprinted 1957, 1959, 1961, 1966, 1969, 1973, 1975, 1976.

A 8.5.a
Fifth edition, first printing: New York: Pocket, [1957].

#2750. 25¢. Wrappers. Reprinted 1963 (A 8.5.b).

A 8.5.c
Fifth edition, third printing: Marlowe. New York: Pocket: [1969].

#75434. 75¢. Wrappers.

A 8.6
Sixth edition: The Second Chandler Omnibus. London: Hamish Hamilton, [1962].

25s. See AA 9.

A 8.7
Seventh edition: New York: Ballantine, [1971].

#02397-8. 95¢. Wrappers. Not seen. Reprinted 1973, 1976. Reprinted in Canada by Ballantine, 1971.

A 8.8
Eighth edition: The Midnight Raymond Chandler. Edited by Joan Kahn. Boston: Houghton Mifflin, 1971.

$10.00. See AA 12.

A 9 THE SIMPLE ART OF MURDER

A 9.1.a
First edition, first printing (1950)

THE SIMPLE ART

of

Murder

by

RAYMOND CHANDLER

HOUGHTON MIFFLIN COMPANY BOSTON
The Riverside Press Cambridge
1 9 5 0

A 9.1.a: 8¹/₁₆″ × 5³/₈″

Copyright, 1934, 1935, 1936, 1938, 1939, 1944, 1950, by Raymond Chandler.
Copyright, 1939, by The Curtis Publishing Company. ◆ The material in this book has
appeared in the following magazines: Black Mask, Dime Detective, Detective Fiction
Weekly, The Saturday Evening Post, Atlantic Monthly, and The Saturday Review of
Literature. ◆ All rights reserved including the right to reproduce this book or parts
thereof in any form.
       ***The Riverside Press,** Cambridge, Massachusetts.   Printed in the U.S.A.*

[i–vi] vii–x [1–2] 3–50 [51–52] 53–90 [91–92] 94–138 [139–140] 141–178 [179–180] 181–219 [220–222] 223–268 [269–270] 271–312 [313–314] 315–330 [331–332] 333–378 [379–380] 381–422 [423–424] 425–464 [465–466] 467–516 [517–518] 519–533 [534]

[1–17]¹⁶

Contents: p. i.: half title; p. ii: 'BY RAYMOND CHANDLER'; p. iii: title; p. iv: coyright; p. v.: 'CONTENTS'; p. vi: blank; pp. vii–x: 'INTRODUCTION'; p. 1: 'FINGER | MAN'; p. 2: blank; pp. 3–533: text; p. 534: blank.
  12 stories: "Introduction," "Finger Man," "Smart-Aleck Kill," "Guns at Cyrano's," "Pick-Up on Noon Street," "Goldfish," "The King in Yellow," "Pearls Are a Nuisance," "I'll Be Waiting," "Red Wind," "Nevada Gas," "Spanish Blood," and "Trouble Is My Business"; and "The Simple Art of Murder." First book appearance of "Pick-Up on Noon Street" and "Introduction." See A 5, A 6, A 7, B 1, C 41, C 42, C 44–C 46, C 48, C 49, C 55, C 56, C 59–61, C 64.

Typography and paper: 6³/₈″ (6⁵/₈″) × 4¹/₈″; 38 or 39 lines per page. Running heads: rectos, story titles; versos, 'THE SIMPLE ART OF MURDER'. Wove paper.

Binding: Fine yellowish gray (#93) B cloth (linen). Front: '[vertical Greek key rule in light yellow (#86)] | [horizontal, dark orange yellow (#72)] THE SIMPLE ART | OF | MURDER'. Spine: '[light yellow Greek key rule] | [dark orange yellow] THE ᒾ SIMPLE | ART | OF | MURDER | CHANDLER | [light yellow Greek key rule] | [dark orange yellow] H.M.CO. | [light yellow Greek key rule]'. White endpapers. All edges trimmed. Top edge stained medium yellow brown.

Dust jacket; Front and spine have illustration in green, blue, red, and white of arms holding palette and brush, log, rope, poison, revolver. Front: '[white] *Raymond* | *Chandler* | [yellow script] The | [yellow roman] SIMPLE ART | OF MURDER | ARTZYBASHEFF'. Spine: '[black] RAYMOND | CHANDLER | [red script] The | [red roman] SIMPLE | ART OF | MURDER | [black against white panel] HOUGHTON | MIFFLIN'. Back: 24-line excerpt from p. 532 of "The Simple Art of Murder" in blue against white. Front flap: blurb in blue against white. Back flap: continuation of blurb and note on Chandler in blue against white.

Publication: 8,000 copies of the first printing. Published 19 September 1950. $3.50.

Printing: Information not available.

Locations: Kent (dj); Lilly (dj).

A 9.1.b
First edition, second printing

The Simple Art | of Murder | [rule] | by | RAYMOND CHANDLER | *With an Editor's Introduction by* | *James Nelson* | [rule] | [Norton device] | W. W. NORTON & COM-PANY • INC. • *New York*

[1950]. $6.95.

The Simple Art of Murder
by Raymond Chandler

The realist in murder writes of a world in which gangsters can rule nations and almost rule cities, in which hotels and apartment houses and celebrated restaurants are owned by men who made their money out of brothels, in which a screen star can be the finger man for a mob, and the nice man down the hall is boss of the numbers racket; a world where a judge with a cellar full of bootleg liquor can send a man to jail for having a pint in his pocket, where the mayor of your town may have condoned murder as an instrument of making money, where no man can walk down a dark street in safety because law and order are things we talk about but refrain from practicing; a world where you may witness a holdup in broad daylight and see who did it, but you will fade quickly back into the crowd rather than tell anyone because the holdup men may have friends with long guns, or the police may not like your testimony, and in any case the shyster for the defense will be allowed to abuse and vilify you in open court, before a jury of selected morons without any but the most perfunctory interference from a political judge. It is not a fragrant world, but it is the world you live in, and certain writers with tough minds and a cool spirit of detachment can make interesting and even amusing patterns out of it.

— From *The Simple Art of Murder*

Dust jacket for A 9.1.a

A 9.2
First English edition, first printing (1950)

The
Simple
Art of
Murder

BY

RAYMOND CHANDLER

HAMISH HAMILTON
LONDON

A 9.2: 7¹/₄″ × 4⁷/₈″

Copyright page: 'Copyright 1950 by Raymond Chandler | *First published in Great Britain, 1950* | *by Hamish Hamilton, Ltd.* | PRINTED IN GREAT BRITAIN BY | WESTERN PRINTING SERVICES LIMITED, BRISTOL'.

[A–B] [i–vi] vii–xi [xii] 1–333 [334–338]

[A]^{16} B–I K–L^{16} (L$_{15-16}$ rear endpapers)

Contents: pp. A–B: blank; p. i: half title; p. ii: *By the same Author'*; p. iii: title; p. iv: copyright; p. v: 'CONTENTS'; p. vi: blank; pp. vii–xi: 'INTRODUCTION'; p. xii: blank; pp. 1–333: text; pp. 334–338: blank (pp. 335–338 are rear endpapers).

7 *stories:* "Introduction," "Finger Man," "Smart-Aleck Kill," "Pick-Up on Noon Street," "The King in Yellow," "Pearls Are a Nuisance," "Nevada Gas," and "Spanish Blood"; and "The Simple Art of Murder." See A 5, A 6, A 7, C 41, C 42, C 44, C 45, C 48, C 56, C 59, C 64.

Note: At 4.1 'customer' should read 'costumer'.

Typography and paper: 5³/₄" (6¹/₈") × 3¹³/₁₆"; 38 lines per page. Running heads: rectos, story titles; versos, 'THE SIMPLE ART OF MURDER'. Wove paper.

Binding: Dark red (#16) V cloth (smooth). Spine goldstamped: 'THE | SIMPLE | ART OF | MURDER | [double rules] | *RAYMOND* | *CHANDLER* | [hh device]'. White endpapers. All edges trimmed.

Dust jacket: Front and spine have illustration of black revolver with yellow and green shadows. Front: '[white swash] The Simple | Art of | [vivid reddish orange swash] Murder | [yellow roman] CWB | [white] RAYMOND CHANDLER'. Spine: '[white swash] The Simple | Art of | [reddish orange swash] Murder | [white] RAYMOND | CHANDLER | Hamish | Hamilton'. Back: quotes reviews of *The Little Sister* in black against white. Front flap: blurb. Back flap: '*Other Books by* | RAYMOND CHANDLER [4 titles]'.

Publication: Unknown number of copies of the first printing. Published 24 November 1950. 10/6.

Printing: See copyright page.

Locations: BL (23 NOV 50); Kent (dj).

A 9.3
Third edition: New York: Pocket, [1953].

Contents: "Introduction," "Pearls Are a Nuisance," "Spanish Blood," "The King in Yellow," "I'll Be Waiting," "The Simple Art of Murder." See A 5, A 6, A 7, C 45, C 56, C 59, C 61, C 64, C 76.

#916. 25¢. Wrappers. 3 printings, 1952–1964.

A 9.4
Fourth edition: New York: Ballantine, [1972].

Contents: "The Simple Art of Murder," "Spanish Blood," "I'll Be Waiting," "The King in Yellow," "Pearls Are a Nuisance." See A 5, A 6, A 7, C 45, C 56, C 59, C 61, C 64.

#02505-9. 95¢. Wrappers. Not seen. Reprinted 1977. Also reprinted in Canada by Ballantine.

Dust jacket for A9.2

A 10 THE LONG GOOD-BYE

A 10.1.a
First edition, first printing (1953)

The Long Good-Bye

BY

RAYMOND CHANDLER

HAMISH HAMILTON

LONDON

A 10.1.a: 7¹/₄″ × 4⁷/₈″

Copyright page: 'First published in Great Britain, 1953 | by Hamish Hamilton Ltd | 90 *Great Russell Street, W.C.* I | | PRINTED IN GREAT BRITAIN BY | EBENEZER BAYLIS AND SON, LTD., THE | TRINITY PRESS, WORCESTER, AND LONDON'.

[1–4] 5–319 [320]

[A] B–I K[16]

Contents: p. 1: half title; p. 2: '*By the same Author*'; p. 3: title page; p. 4: copyright page; pp. 5–320: text.

Typography and paper: $5^{3}/_{4}''$ (6") × $3^{7}/_{8}''$; 38 lines per page. No running heads. Wove paper.

Binding: Dark grayish red (#20) paper-covered boards with V grain. Spine silver-stamped: 'THE | LONG | GOOD- | BYE | [short thick and thin rules] | *RAYMOND* | *CHANDLER* | [hh device]'. White endpapers. All edges trimmed.

Dust jacket: Front and spine have illustration in shades of blue, green, red, and yellow of open doorway showing naked woman in bed. Front: '[yellow] THE LONG | GOOD-BYE | [white] Raymond Chandler'. Spine: '[light gray] Raymond | Chandler | [yellow] THE | LONG | GOOD | BYE | [greenish blue] HAMISH | HAMILTON'. Back: quotes from reviews of *The Raymond Chandler Omnibus, TSAOM, TLS.* Front flap: blurb. Back flap: quotes from reviews of *TLITL, THW, FML, TBS.*

Publication: Unknown number of copies of the first printing. Published 27 November 1953. 10/6. Copyright 17 November 1953.

Printing: See copyright page.

Locations: BL (16 NOV 53); Kent (dj); Lilly (dj).

Note: See Robert M. Miller, "The Publication of Raymond Chandler's *The Long Goodbye*," *Papers of the Bibliographical Society of America,* LXIII (4th Quarter 1969), 279–290. Miller notes 86 textual variants between the first and second Hamish Hamilton printings. The first printing of the Houghton Mifflin edition incorporated 65 of the alterations in the second Hamish Hamilton printing and introduced 64 new substantive readings.

A 10.1.b
First edition, second printing: London: Hamish Hamilton, [1953].

Copyright page: '*Second Impression December, 1953*'.

A 10.1.c
First edition, third printing: London: Thriller Book Club, [   ].

Not seen.

A 10.1.d
Fourth edition, fourth printing: London: Hamish Hamilton, [1971].

A Fingerprint Book. Reprinted 1971, 1976.

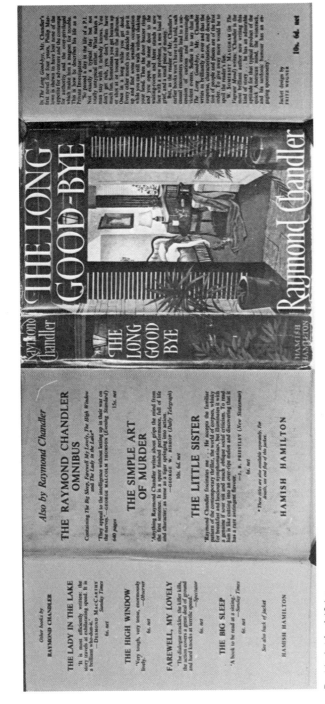

Dust jacket for A10.1.a

A 10.2.a
First American edition, first printing (1954)

The Long Goodbye

RAYMOND   CHANDLER

HOUGHTON MIFFLIN COMPANY
BOSTON · · The Riverside Press Cambridge

1954

A 10.2.a: 8¹/₁₆″ × 5⁷/₁₆″

First published in the United States, 1954.

Copyright, 1953, by Raymond Chandler
All rights reserved including the right to reproduce
this book or parts thereof in any form

Library of Congress Catalogue Card No. 54-5278

★

𝕿𝖍𝖊 𝕽𝖎𝖛𝖊𝖗𝖘𝖎𝖉𝖊 𝕻𝖗𝖊𝖘𝖘
CAMBRIDGE · MASSACHUSETTS

Printed in the U.S.A.

[i–iv] [1] 2–316

[1^8] [2–10]^{16} [11]^8

Contents: p. i: half title; p. ii: 'BY RAYMOND CHANDLER'; p. iii: title page; p. iv: copyright page; pp. 1–316: text.

Typography and paper: 6^1/$_4$″ (6^9/$_{16}$″) × 4^1/$_8$″; 38 lines per page. No running heads. Wove paper.

Binding: 3-piece binding: half of front and back in medium yellowish green (#136) V cloth (smooth); spine and other half of front and back in medium blue (#182). Front: '[vivid dark yellowish green (#138)] The Long | Goodbye'. Spine: '[vertical] [vivid dark yellowish green] The Long Goodbye CHANDLER | [horizontal] H.M.CO.' White endpapers. All edges trimmed. Top edge stained medium yellowish green.

Dust jacket: Front and spine in bluish gray and dark reddish brown, with green eye, bloody tan statue, figure carrying suitcase, hair, and vial of red pills. Front: '[yellow] *the* Long | Goodbye | a novel by | [white] *Raymond* | *Chandler* | [pale green] LORRAINE'. Spine: '[yellow] *the* | Long | Good- | bye | [white] *Chandler* | [yellow] HMCo'. Back: '[blue against white] THERE ARE BLONDES— [30 lines from pp. 74– 75]'. Front flap: blurb. Back flap: continuation of blurb.

Publication: 10,000 copies of the first printing. Published 18 March 1954. $3.00. Copyright 1 March 1954. Copyright #A128517.

Printing: Composed, printed, and bound by Houghton Mifflin, Cambridge, Mass.

Locations: Kent (dj); LC (MAR-5 1954, rebound); Lilly (dj).

A 10.2.b
First American edition, second printing: Boston: Houghton Mifflin [1954].

The second printing removes the date from the title page.

A 10.3
Third edition: Boston: Houghton Mifflin, [1954].

'BOOK CLUB EDITION' specified on front flap of dust jacket. July 1954 selection of the Literary Guild.

A 10.4
Fourth edition: Reading-For-Men. Garden City: Literary Guild, [1954].

Wrappers.

Dust jacket for A 10.2.a

A 10.5
Fifth edition: New York: Pocket, [1955].

#1044. 25¢. Wrappers. 4 printings, 1955–1964.

A 10.6
Sixth edition: [Harmondsworth]: Penguin/in association with Hamish Hamilton, [1959].

#1400. 3/6. Wrappers. Reprinted 1961, 1963, 1966, 1971, 1973, 1974, 1976.

A 10.7
Seventh edition: The Second Chandler Omnibus. London: Hamish Hamilton, [1962].

25s. See AA 9.

A 10.8
Eighth edition: New York: Ballantine, [1971].

#02396-X-095. 95¢. Wrappers. Reprinted 1972, 1973 (twice), 1976. Possible 1971 Canadian printing.

A 10.9
Ninth edition: The Midnight Raymond Chandler. Edited by Joan Kahn. Boston: Houghton Mifflin, 1971.

$10.00 See AA 12.

A 10.10
Tenth edition: London: Hutchinson Educational, 1974.

Adapted by Patrick Nobes. Wrappers.

A 11 PLAYBACK

A 11.1.a
First edition, first printing (1958)

Playback

BY

RAYMOND CHANDLER

HAMISH HAMILTON
LONDON

A 11.1.a: $7^3/_{16}'' \times 4^{13}/_{16}''$

Copyright page: 'First published in Great Britain, 1958 | by Hamish Hamilton Ltd. | 90 *Great Russell Street London WC* 1 | *Copyright* © 1958 *by Raymond Chandler* | PRINTED IN GREAT BRITAIN BY | EBENEZER BAYLIS AND SON, LTD., THE | TRINITY PRESS, WORCESTER, AND LONDON'.

[1–6] 7–207 [208]

[A]⁸ B–G¹⁶

Contents: p. 1: half title; p. 2: *'By the same Author'*; p. 3: title page; p. 4: copyright page; p. 5: 'TO | JEAN AND HELGA | without whom this book would | never have been written'; p. 6: blank; pp. 7–208: text.

Typography and paper: 5⁹/₁₆″ (5³/₄″) × 3¹/₂″; 31 lines per page. No running heads. Wove paper.

Binding: Two bindings noted. Deep reddish orange (#36) paper-covered boards with BF grain (fine bead-grain). Spine silverstamped: '[tapered rule with dot] | PLAY- | BACK | [tapered rule with dot] | Raymond | Chandler | [HH device]'. Also stamped in vivid yellow (#82) with smaller hh device. White endpapers. All edges trimmed.

Dust jacket: Front and spine printed against black. Front: '[tapered yellow rule with dot] | [white and red] PLAYBACK | [tapered yellow rule with dot] | [white] Raymond | Chandler'. Spine: '[tapered yellow rule with dot] | [white and red] PLAY- | BACK | [tapered yellow rule with dot] | [white] Raymond | Chandler | [red hh device]'. Back: photo of Chandler by Douglas Glass. Front flap: blurb. Back flap: continuation of blurb and 'Also by RAYMOND CHANDLER'.

Publication: Unknown number of copies of the first printing. Published 10 July 1958. 12/6.

Printing: See copyright page.

Locations: BL (1 JUL 1958, silverstamped); Kent (silverstamped, dj); Lilly (both bindings, dj).

Note: Abridged in *Suspense*, 1 (October 1958), 130–160; (November 1958), 126–160. Also in *Personality* (4 December 1958), 76–77, 97–105; (18 December 1958), 64–69; (1 January 1959), 50–54, 65–70; (15 January 1959), 42–45. See C 96, F 7.

Review copy

Book sheets bound in printed light greenish yellow (#101) wrappers. Front: *'Playback* | [tapered rule] | BY | RAYMOND CHANDLER | [rest of front wrapper covered by printed label which extends over spine and part of back]'. Spine: '[vertical, up] Hamish Hamilton PLAYBACK'. Label: '[brown against white] [wavy rules] | Hamish Hamilton Ltd | *90 GREAT RUSSELL STREET LONDON WCI* | UNCORRECTED PROOF | *Title* [typed] PLAYBACK | *Author* [typed] Raymond Chandler | *Probable Price* [typed] 12s.6d. | *Probable Publication Date* [typed] July, 1958 | [wavy rules]'.

Location: Kent.

A 11.1.b
First edition, second printing: London: Thriller Book Club, [1958?].

A 11.1.c
First edition, third printing: London: Hamish Hamilton, [1973].

A Fingerprint Book.

PLAYBACK

Raymond Chandler

RAYMOND CHANDLER

Douglas Glass

Photograph on back of jacket by
Douglas Glass

Jacket design by
PATRICIA DAVEY

12s. 6d.

In Playback, after it far too long Goodbye, Philip Marlowe is back...

(continued on back flap)

(continued from front flap)

Also by RAYMOND CHANDLER

THE BIG SLEEP	7s. 6d.
FAREWELL, MY LOVELY	7s. 6d.
THE HIGH WINDOW	7s. 6d.
THE LADY IN THE LAKE	7s. 6d.
THE LITTLE SISTER	7s. 6d.
PEARLS ARE A NUISANCE	7s. 6d.
SMART-ALECK KILL	7s. 6d.

RAYMOND CHANDLER OMNIBUS
(containing The Big Sleep, Farewell,
My Lovely, The High Window and
The Lady in the Lake) 18s.

Dust jacket for A 11.1.a

Playback

BY
RAYMOND CHANDLER

Hamish Hamilton Ltd

90 GREAT RUSSELL STREET LONDON WC1

UNCORRECTED PROOF

Title   PLAYBACK

Author   Raymond Chandler

Probable Price   12s.6d.

Probable Publication Date   July,1958

Front wrapper of A11.1.a review copy

A 11.2.a
First American edition, first printing (1958)

PLAYBACK

BY
RAYMOND
CHANDLER

1958

HOUGHTON MIFFLIN COMPANY BOSTON
THE RIVERSIDE PRESS CAMBRIDGE

A 11.2.a: 8″ × 5⁷/₁₆″

Copyright © 1958 by Raymond Chandler

All rights reserved including the right to
reproduce this book or parts thereof in any form

Library of Congress Catalog Card Number: 58–9057

First Printing

Printed in the U.S.A.

[i–viii] [1] 2–205 [206–208]; first page of each chapter unnumbered.

Perfect binding.

Contents: p. i: half title; p. ii: 'BOOKS BY | RAYMOND CHANDLER'; p. iii: title page; p. iv: copyright page; p. v: 'To Jean and Helga'; p. vi: blank; p vii: half title; p. viii: blank; pp. 1–205: text; pp. 206–208: blank.

Typography and paper: 5¹³/₁₆″ (6¹/₁₆″) × 3¹³/₁₆″; 30 lines per page. No running heads. Wove paper.

Binding: Medium orange (#53) V cloth (smooth); front and spine stamped in deep brown (#56). Front: '[within 7 concentric circles and completing bottom of eighth] PLAYBACK'. Spine: '[vertical] [2 rules] Raymond Chandler [rule] PLAYBACK [rule] H. M. CO. [2 rules]'. White endpapers. Top and bottom edges trimmed. Top edge stained brown.

Dust jacket: Front and spine lettered against design in black, white, blue green, and shades of dark purple—perhaps intended to suggest movie frames. Front: '[olive brown half of movie reel] [white against purple panel] Raymond | CHANDLER | [black against yellowish brown movie reel] PLAYBACK | A Philip Marlowe Story'. Spine: '[vertical] [white against purple panels] PLAYBACK | [1 line below] chandler | h.m.co.'. Back: '[black against white background] Raymond Chandler [33-line biographical note]'. Front flap: blurb. Back flap: continuation of blurb.

Publication: 6,000 copies of the first printing. Published 16 October 1958. $3.00. Copyright 23 September 1958. Copyright #A357382.

Printing: Manufactured by Houghton Mifflin, Cambridge, Mass., and H. Wolff, New York City.

Locations: Kent (dj); LC (OCT-3 1958).

A 11.2.b
First American edition, second printing: Boston: Houghton Mifflin, [1958].

Not seen.

A 11.2.c
First American edition, third printing: Boston: Houghton Mifflin, [1958].

Copyright page: 'THIRD PRINTING'.

A 11.3
Third edition: Boston: Houghton Mifflin, [1958].

'Doubleday Book Club' specified on front flap of dust jacket.

$3.00

Raymond
CHANDLER

PLAYBACK

Readers who have been waiting since *The Long Goodbye* for a new Raymond Chandler novel will now find Philip Marlowe, Private Investigator, back again — as tough, as ingratiating, and above all as keen-eyed as ever.

When Marlowe receives an arrogant phone call from Attorney Clyde Umney engaging his services as PI to meet the Super Chief in Los Angeles, his well known curiosity is aroused — particularly since the passenger to be met is a voluptuous redhead. But the work begins to wonder whether he should have taken the case blind. What is Betty Mayfield's angle? Is she on the downhill tramp? A criminal? A spoiled little rich girl? Who is getting the short end of the deal ...

continued on next top

PLAYBACK
chandler

Raymond CHANDLER
PLAYBACK

h.m.co.

Raymond Chandler

Writing is his business, and he learned the trade by feeling his way in the pulps and slicks. A realist in murder, unconcerned with the whodunit or thriller, his aim is to impart the right emotion to the right nerves and to set down combinations of words that can get up and walk.

Read him, study him, and beneath the astringent cynicism and the sardonic humor you will find an uncompromising integrity. Against anything, that smells of exploitation and debasement, he is at the opposite pole from the character of whom he wrote: "His standard of ethics would take about as much strain as a very tired old cobweb."

He admires the art of Chaplin, applauds the revival of Scott Fitzgerald, and acknowledges his debt to Dashiell Hammett.

His attitude toward his publishers is refreshing: I write 'em, you sell 'em. And he says he doesn't like the silly face of authors on book jackets, including his own.

He had Quaker ancestors on both sides (Now what do you make of that, Marlowe?) He was born in Chicago (Marlowe nods with approval), and grew up in England (Marlowe assumes a quizzical air). For four or five years he studied Latin and Greek at Dulwich College and a decade or two later, J B Priestley first looked into the Chandler shadow and exclaimed: "They never wrote like this at Dulwich."

Although he knows his way around that "mean lighted slum known as Hollywood," Chandler has never been a barkeep, set up pins in a bowling alley, or played the game politely termed blackmail. He wouldn't be caught dead in a nightclub and no dick would bother to look at him twice. He declines to say whether or not he returns the compliment.

continued from inner top

lawyers, or Betty herself? When he wakes up in a motel bedroom with a badly battered skull, Marlowe realizes he had better be quick to find out the right answers to these questions.

The unraveling of the mystery takes him along the Southern California coast where he meets the full complement of remarkable Raymond Chandler characters — from Helen Vermilyea, a glamorous secretary with a well-cherished head of platinum hair, to Henry Clarendon IV, old, rich, aristocratic, and very, very observant.

As always, Marlowe is capable of handling unexpected situations in an unexpected way. *Playback* is Raymond Chandler at his very best.

Jacket by
Richard J L Tihak

Dust jacket for A11.2.a

A 11.4
Fourth edition: New York: Pocket, [1960].

#C-375. 35¢. Wrappers.

A 11.5
Fifth edition: [Harmondsworth]: Penguin/in association with Hamish Hamilton, [1961].

#1608. 2/6. Wrappers. Reprinted 1963, 1965, 1971, 1973, 1975.

A 11.6
Sixth edition: The Second Chandler Omnibus. London: Hamish Hamilton, [1962].

25s. See AA 9.

A 11.7
Seventh edition: New York: Pyramid, [1968].

#X-1889. 60¢. Wrappers.

A 11.8
Eighth edition: New York: Ballantine, [1977].

#25169. $1.50. Wrappers. Also reprinted in Canada by Ballantine.

A 12 RAYMOND CHANDLER ON WRITING
Only edition (1962)

Raymond Chandler

on

Writing

From *Raymond Chandler Speaking,* **edited by Dorothy Gardiner and Kathrine Sorley Walker, to be published by Houghton Mifflin Company in April, 1962.**

A 12: 8³/₄″ × 5³/₄″

From *Raymond Chandler Speaking*, edited by
Dorothy Gardiner and Kathrine Sorley Walker,
to be published by Houghton Mifflin Company.
Copyright © 1962 by the Helga Greene Literary
Agency. All rights reserved. Printed in the U.S.A.

[i–ii] [1] 2–23 [24–26]

[1]^{14}

Contents: p. i (front wrapper): title page; p. ii: copyright page; pp. 1–23: text; p. 24: blank; p. 25: '*Books by Raymond Chandler* [8 titles]'; p. 26 (back wrapper): blank.
    Text: Material from *Raymond Chandler Speaking.* See A 13.1.b.

Paper: White wove paper.

Binding: Cover title; self-wrappers. Stapled.

Publication: Unknown number of copies published before April 1962 as promotional pamphlet for *Raymond Chandler Speaking.* Not for sale.

Location: Kent.

A 13 RAYMOND CHANDLER SPEAKING

A 13.1.a
First edition, first printing (1962)

Raymond Chandler
Speaking

EDITED BY

DOROTHY GARDINER

AND

KATHRINE SORLEY WALKER

Illustrated

HAMISH HAMILTON
LONDON

A 13.1.a: $8^{1}/_{2}'' \times 5^{7}/_{16}''$

Copyright page: 'First published in Great Britain, 1962 | by Hamish Hamilton Ltd | 90 Great Russell Street London WC1 | Copyright © 1962 by the Helga Greene Literary Agency | PRINTED IN GREAT BRITAIN | BY WESTERN PRINTING SERVICES LTD, BRISTOL'.

[1–9] 10–11 [12] 13–15 [16–19] 20–43 [44–47] 48–70 [71–73] 74–95 [96–99] 100–112 [113–115] 116–144 [145–147] 148–173 [174–177] 178–184 [185–187] 188–204 [205–207] 208–249 [250–253] 254–271 [272]; 5 glossy photos inserted.

[A] B–H¹⁶ I⁸

Contents: p. 1: half title; p. 2: *'By the same author'*; p. 3: title page; p. 4: copyright page; p. 5: *'ACKNOWLEDGMENTS'*; p. 6: blank; p. 7: *'CONTENTS'*; p. 8: *'ILLUSTRA-TIONS'*; pp. 9–11: *'Foreword* | BY | DOROTHY GARDINER'; pp. 12–15: *'Raymond Chandler: Curriculum Vitae'*; p. 16: blank; p. 17: 'CHANDLER ON CHANDLER'; p. 18: blank; pp. 19–264: text; pp. 265–271: *'Index'*; p. 272: blank.

  Text: "Chandler on Chandler," "Chandler on the Mystery Novel" ("Casual Notes on the Mystery Novel"), "Chandler on the Craft of Writing" ("From Chandler's Working Notebook: Notes on English and American Style"), "A Couple of Writers," "Chandler on the Film World and Television" ("Writers in Hollywood," "Extract from Notes Dated 1950 About the Screenplay *Strangers on a Train*"), "Chandler on Publishing" ("Ten Per Cent of Your Life"), "Chandler on Cats," "Chandler on Famous Crimes" ("The Maybrick Case," "The Crippen Case," "The Wallace Case," "The Bartlett Case"), "Chandler on His Novels, Short Stories and Philip Marlowe" ("1939 Plan of Work Taken from Chandler's Notebook"), "The Poodle Springs Story." See A 17, C 65, C 79, C 101.

Typography and paper: 6⅝" (6⅞") × 4"; 40 or 42 lines per page. Running heads: rectos, section titles; versos, *'Raymond Chandler Speaking'*. Wove paper.

Binding: Vivid deep purple red (blue and red dots) (#257) paper-covered boards with V grain. Spine goldstamped: '[line of dots] | Raymond | Chandler | Speaking | [line of dots] | [hh device]'. White endpapers. All edges trimmed.

Dust jacket: Front: '[white against purple panel] RAYMOND | CHANDLER | [follow-ing against yellowish green panel] [black] *speaking* | [left column: photo of Chandler] | *edited by Dorothy Gardiner* | *& Kathrine Sorley Walker* [right column: 21 lines in black]'. Spine: '[vertical] [white against purple panel] RAYMOND | [1 line below] CHANDLER | [black against yellowish green panel] *speaking* | [horizontal] [black] Hamish | Hamilton'. Back: '[black against white] *What the Critics have said about* [excerpts from reviews]'. Front flap: blurb. Back flap: 'RAYMOND CHANDLER'S | Novels and Stories [10 titles]'.

Publication: Unknown number of copies of the first printing. Published 15 March 1962. 21s.

Printing: See copyright page.

Locations: BL (7 MAR 62); Kent (dj).

Review copy

Book sheets bound in printed yellow wrappers. Title page: *'Raymond Chandler* | *Speaking* | *EDITED BY* | DOROTHY GARDINER | *AND* | KATHRINE SORLEY WALKER | *Illustrated* | [hh device] | HAMISH HAMILTON | LONDON'.

Location: Helga Greene Agency.

RAYMOND CHANDLER
CHANDLER
speaking

RAYMOND
CHANDLER speaking

Creator of Philip Marlowe and
author of some of the best
dialogue ever written, Raymond
Chandler was a vivid and
inveterate letter-writer. This
book, consisting mainly of
letters from Chandler to his
friends, contains some of his
pithiest writing. It also includes the first chapters of
his unfinished novel and other
unpublished writings. Here, too,
are his uninhibited views on:

Philip Marlowe
Real-life murders
Hollywood
The mystery novel
Cats
Publishers
Television
The craft of writing

*edited by Dorothy Gardiner
& Kathrine Sorley Walker*

Hamish
Hamilton

Raymond Chandler, creator of Philip
Marlowe and author of some of the
best dialogue ever written in America,
was an inveterate and vivid letter-
writer. This book, consisting mainly
of letters from Chandler to his friends,
contains some of his pithiest writing
about the technique of the mystery
story, Hollywood, television, publishers, cats, literary agents and many
other subjects on which his opinions
were always shrewd, often witty,
sometimes cantankerous and now
and again explosive.

Besides this wide selection from his
letters, the book contains the first four
chapters of the book on which he was
at work when he died in 1959, his
notes on several real-life murders and
a number of examples of his writing
never published in book form before.

*The photograph on the front of the jacket
appeared by courtesy of the late Bill Courtaine and was
reproduced in the Sunday Times.*

RAYMOND CHANDLER'S
Novels and Stories

THE BIG SLEEP   7s. 6d. net
FAREWELL, MY LOVELY 7s. 6d. net
THE HIGH WINDOW   7s. 6d. net
THE LADY IN THE LAKE 7s. 6d. net

All the above are also contained in
THE RAYMOND CHANDLER
OMNIBUS 25s. net

THE LITTLE SISTER   7s. 6d. net
THE LONG GOODBYE   7s. 6d. net
PLAYBACK   12s. 6d. net
PEARLS ARE A NUISANCE 7s. 6d. net
SMART-ALECK KILL   7s. 6d. net

What the Critics have said about
RAYMOND CHANDLER'S
books—

'Mr Raymond Chandler seems to me the best American detective-story
writer in the tough and terse Dashiell Hammett tradition.'
J. B. PRIESTLEY

'Raymond Chandler is not out-and-out most detective-story writer—he is
a craftsman so brilliant, he has an imagination so wholly original, that
no connoisseur of modern American literature ought, I think, to
exclude him.'—ELIZABETH BOWEN (*Tatler*)

'Raymond Chandler has informed the murder of Dashiell Hammett and
dyed it a deeper shade of crimson.'—*Morning Recreation (Observer)*

and films

'Chandler's writing is at its best sharply visual, getting its effects by
observed detail, the small shocking thing seen. Farewell, My Lovely
is the first serious attempt at putting on the screen his peculiar mixture
of hardness, sensuality, high polish and backstreet poetry — for
poetry, I protest, is there.'—DILYS POWELL Sunday Times

'Anyone who has read Mr Chandler's thrillers knows that he can write
well.'—A. A. Lejeune Observer

'Chandler has done it again. His film, The Blue Dahlia, is a thriller
with characters sharply etched, an ingenious plot, exciting incident and
larceny out it has, indeed, all the characteristics of his books.'
Campbell Dixon (Daily Telegraph)

HAMISH HAMILTON

A 13.1.b
First edition, first American printing (1962)

Raymond Chandler
Speaking

EDITED BY

DOROTHY GARDINER

AND

KATHRINE SORLEY WALKER

illustrated with photographs

1962

HOUGHTON MIFFLIN COMPANY BOSTON
The Riverside Press, Cambridge

A 13.1.b: 8³/₈″ × 5³/₄″

First Printing

Copyright © 1962 by the Helga Greene Literary Agency
All rights reserved including the right to reproduce this
book or parts thereof in any form
Library of Congress Catalog Card Number: 62-8125

The Riverside Press
Cambridge • Massachusetts
Printed in the U.S.A.

[A–B] [1–9] 10–11 [12] 13–15 [16–19] 20–26 [C–D] 27–34 [E–F] 35–43 [44–47] 48–70 [71–73] 74–78 [G–H] 79–95 [96–99] 100–112 [113–115] 116–144 [145–147] 148–173 [174–177] 178–182 [I–J] 183–184 [185–187] 188–204 [205–207] 208–249 [250–253] 254–271 [272–278]; illustrations integral.

Perfect binding.

Contents: Same as first Hamish Hamilton printing except: pp. 272–278: blank.

Typography and paper: Same as first Hamish Hamilton printing.

Binding: Grayish blue (#186) V cloth (smooth); front and spine stamped in deep red (#13). Front: '[within angular box of single rules] Raymond | Chandler | Speaking'. Spine: '[vertical] Raymond Chandler Speaking | [horizontal] Gardiner | *and* | Sorley | Walker | HMCO'. White endpapers. Top and bottom edges trimmed. Yellow, blue, and green bands at top and bottom.

Dust jacket: Front and spine lettered against dark yellow. Front: '[3 lines within angular white panel] [red] Raymond | [green] Chandler | [blue] Speaking | [white] . . . on the making of | detectives, | the writing of novels, TV and cats, | at ease in the wisest | and toughest of letters. | [red] Edited by DOROTHY GARDINER and KATHRINE SORLEY WALKER'. Spine: '[vertical] [red] Raymond | [green] Chandler [blue] Speaking | [horizontal] [red] GARDINER | and | SORLEY | WALKER | [white] HMCO'. Back: '[blue against white] except from RAYMOND | CHANDLER | SPEAKING [25 lines]'. Front flap: blurb. Back flap: continuation of blurb.

Publication: 7,500 copies of the first Houghton Mifflin printing. Published 24 April 1962. $4.00. Copyright 9 March 1962. Copyright #A55245.

Printing: Produced by the Riverside Press, Cambridge, Mass., and Halliday Lithograph, West Hanover, Mass.

Locations: Kent (dj); LC (MAR 15 1962).

A 13.1.c
First edition, third printing: London: Hamish Hamilton, [1962].

Not seen.

A 13.1.d
First edition, fourth printing: Boston: Houghton Mifflin, [1962].

Copyright page: 'Second Printing'.

A 13.1.e
First edition, fifth printing: Plainview, N.Y.: Books for Libraries, [1971].

Dust jacket for A 13.1.b

A 13.1.f
First edition, sixth printing: London: Hamish Hamilton Library, [1973].

£2.50.

A 13.1.g
First edition, seventh printing: Boston: Houghton Mifflin, 1977.

$5.95. Wrappers.

A 13.2
Second edition: [London]: Four Square, [1966].

#1493. 5s. Wrappers.

A 14 KILLER IN THE RAIN

A 14.1.a
First edition, first printing (1964)

KILLER IN THE RAIN

BY

RAYMOND CHANDLER

WITH AN INTRODUCTION BY

PHILIP DURHAM

HAMISH HAMILTON
LONDON

A 14.1.a: 8¹/₄″ × 5³/₈″

Copyright page: 'First Published in Great Britain 1964 | by Hamish Hamilton Ltd. | 90 Great Russell Street, London, W.C. 1. | Copyright © 1964 Helga Greene Literary Agency | PRINTED IN GREAT BRITAIN | BY EBENEZER BAYLIS AND SON, LIMITED | THE TRINITY PRESS, WORCESTER, AND LONDON'.

[i–vi] vii–xi [xii] [1–2] 3–37 [38–40] 41–72 [73–74] 75–106 [107–108] 109–141 [142–144] 145–186 [187–188] 189–240 [241–242] 243–282 [283–284] 285–332

[1]^{16} 2–10^{16} 11^8 12^4

Contents: p. i: half title; p. ii: *'The Works of Raymond Chandler';* p. iii: title; p. iv: copyright; p. v: 'CONTENTS'; p. vi: blank; pp. vii–xi: 'INTRODUCTION'; p. xii: blank; p. 1: half title; p. 2: blank; pp. 3–332: text.

    8 stories: *"Killer in the Rain," "The Man Who Liked Dogs," *"The Curtain," *"Try the Girl," *"Mandarin's Jade," *"Bay City Blues," *"The Lady in the Lake," "No Crime in the Mountains." Asterisks indicate first book publication. See B3, B6, C43, C47, C50, C51, C54, C57, C58, C63.

Typography and paper: 6^{13}/₁₆″ (7″) × 4¹/₈″; 45 lines per page. Running heads: rectos and versos, story titles. Wove paper.

Binding: Dark red (#16) paper-covered boards with V grain. Spine goldstamped: 'Killer | in the | Rain | [rule] | *RAYMOND | CHANDLER* | [hh device]'. White endpapers. All edges trimmed.

Dust jacket: Front: '[against dark blue panel with dagger outlined in black and raindrops] [white] KILLER | IN | THE | RAIN | [against dark grayish yellow panel with raindrops] [white] *RAYMOND | CHANDLER | ANDREW'*. Spine: '[vertical against dark blue panel with raindrops] [white] KILLER IN THE RAIN [against dark grayish yellow panel with raindrops] *RAYMOND CHANDLER* | [horizontal hh seal in white]'. Back: critical comments on Chandler's books and movies. Front flap: blurb. Back flap: 'RAYMOND CHANDLER'S | Novels and Stories [11 titles]'.

Publication: Unknown number of copies of the first printing. Published 26 March 1964. 21s.

Printing: See copyright page.

Locations: BL (16 MAR 64); Kent (dj); Lilly (dj).

Review copy

Book sheets bound in yellow printed wrappers. Title page: 'KILLER | IN THE | RAIN | [hh device] | HAMISH HAMILTON | LONDON'.

Location: Helga Greene Agency.

A 14.1.b
First edition, second printing: London: Hamish Hamilton, 1964.

Not seen.

A 14.1.c
First edition, third printing: London: Quality Book Club, [1964].

On copyright page: 'Third Impression, December 1964'.

A 14.1.d
First edition, fourth printing: London: Hamish Hamilton, [1970].

A Fingerprint Book. Reprinted 1973.

KILLER IN THE RAIN

RAYMOND CHANDLER

KILLER IN THE RAIN · RAYMOND CHANDLER

RAYMOND CHANDLER

RAYMOND CHANDLER used to call these stories, most of which has been published in England before, his 'cannibalised' work. By this he meant that in later life he removed usable characters and situations from them in the full-length novels which made him famous.

Most of them first appeared in the famous magazine *Black Mask* when Chandler and Dashiell Hammett both learned their craft. They read to the Chandler fan, as he reads them, to get a touch of early pleasure; the non-addict a triple pleasure: thrilling scenes of plot and dialogue he has met before in, say, *The Big Sleep*, and recognising with what ingenious variation Chandler put them to fresh uses.

The eight stories are "Killer in the Rain," "Try the Girl," "No Crime in the Mountains," "Mandarin's Jade," "The Lady in the Lake," "Try the Girl," "The Curtain" and "The Man Who Liked Dogs."

There is a Foreword by Philip Durham, who has written the Introduction, teaches at the University of California, Los Angeles, where there is a large collection of Chandler manuscripts.

21s.
net

Jacket design by
NOEL ANDREW

What the Critics have said about
RAYMOND CHANDLER'S

books—

'Mr. Raymond Chandler seems to me the best American detective-story writer in the tough and tense Dashiell Hammett tradition.'
J. B. PRIESTLEY

'Raymond Chandler is not just one more detective-story writer—he is a craftsman so brilliant, he has an imagination so wholly original, that no consideration of modern American literature ought, I think, to exclude him.'—ELIZABETH BOWEN (*Tatler*)

'Raymond Chandler has inherited the mantle of Dashiell Hammett and dyed it a deeper shade of crimson.'
MAURICE RICHARDSON (*Observer*)

and films

'Chandler's writing is at its best sharply visual, getting its effects by observed detail, the small shocking thing seen. *Farewell, My Lovely* is the first serious attempt at putting on the screen his peculiar mixture of harshness, sensuality, high polish and backstreet poetry ... for poetry, I persist, is there.'
DILYS POWELL (*Sunday Times*)

'Anyone who has read Mr. Chandler's thrillers knows that he can write well'—C. A. LEJEUNE (*Observer*)

'Chandler has done it again. His film, *The Blue Dahlia*, is a thriller with characters sharply etched, an ingenious plot, exciting incident and laconic wit. It has, indeed, all the characteristics of his books.'
CAMPBELL DIXON (*Daily Telegraph*)

RAYMOND CHANDLER'S

Novels and Stories

FAREWELL, MY LOVELY 7s. 6d. net
THE HIGH WINDOW 7s. 6d. net
THE LADY IN THE LAKE 7s. 6d. net

These three books, together with THE BIG SLEEP, *are also contained in*

THE RAYMOND CHANDLER OMNIBUS 25s. net

THE LITTLE SISTER 7s. 6d. net
PLAYBACK 12s. 6d. net

These two books, together with THE LONG GOOD-BYE, *and* THE SIMPLE ART OF MURDER, *are also contained in*

THE SECOND CHANDLER OMNIBUS 25s. net

PEARLS ARE A NUISANCE 7s. 6d. net
SMART-ALECK KILL 7s. 6d. net

and

KILLER IN THE RAIN 25s. net

Also:

RAYMOND CHANDLER SPEAKING

Edited by Dorothy Gardiner and Katherine Sorley Walker

Illustrated 18s. net

HAMISH HAMILTON

Dust jacket for A 14.1.a

A 14.2
First American edition, only printing (1964)

KILLER
IN THE
RAIN

RAYMOND CHANDLER

With an Introduction by Philip Durham

HOUGHTON MIFFLIN COMPANY BOSTON
THE RIVERSIDE PRESS CAMBRIDGE

1 9 6 4

A 14.2: 8³/₈″ × 5⁵/₈″

FIRST PRINTING   C

Copyright © 1964 by Helga Greene Literary Agency

*All rights reserved including the right to reproduce
this book or parts thereof in any form*

"Killer in the Rain," "The Man Who Liked Dogs," "The Curtain,"
and "Try the Girl" were first published in the magazine *Black
Mask*. Copyright 1934, 1936 by Pro-Distributors Publishing Company. "Mandarin's Jade," "Bay City Blues," and "The Lady in the
Lake" originally appeared in *Dime Detective Magazine*. Copyright
1937, 1938 by Popular Publications. "No Crime in the Mountains"
first appeared in *Detective Story Magazine*. Copyright 1941 by
Street and Smith.

LIBRARY OF CONGRESS CATALOG CARD NUMBER: 64-17361

PRINTED IN THE U.S.A.

[A–B] [i–vii] viii–xii [xiii–xiv] [1] 2–41 [42–45] 46–81 [82–85] 86–123 [124–127]
128–165 [166–169] 170–219 [220–223] 224–283 [284–287] 288–334 [335–337]
338–394 [395–400]

[1–13]¹⁶

Contents: pp. A–B: blank; p. i: half title; p. ii: *'Also by Raymond Chandler';* p. iii: title;
p. iv: copyright; p. v: 'CONTENTS'; p. vi: blank; pp. vii–xii: 'INTRODUCTION'; p. xiii:
half title; p. xiv: blank; pp. 1–394: text; pp. 395–400: blank.
  8 stories: Same as Hamish Hamilton edition.

Typography and paper: 6⁵/₈″ (6⁷/₈″) × 4¹/₈″; 39 or 40 lines per page. Running heads:
rectos and versos, story titles. Wove paper.

Binding: Dark blue (#183) V cloth (smooth); front and spine stamped in white. Front:
'KILLER | IN THE | RAIN'. Spine: '[umbrella] | KILLER | IN THE | RAIN | CHANDLER
| HMCO'. White endpapers. All edges trimmed. Blue and white bands at top and
bottom.

Dust jacket: Front: '[against dark blue and black background with man holding um-
brella and pistol] [brilliant yellow green] killer | in | the | rain | [white] raymond
chandler'. Spine: '[against dark blue and black background] [brilliant yellow green]
killer | in | the | rain | [vertical] [white] Raymond Chandler | [horizontal] [white]
Houghton | Mifflin | Company'. Back: photo of Chandler with cat. Front flap: blurb.
Back: continuation of blurb and note on Chandler.

Publication: 5,000 copies of the first printing. Published 9 September 1964. $5.50.
Copyright #AI-9048.

Printing: Produced by the Riverside Press, Cambridge, Mass.

Location: Kent (dj).

killer in the rain

Raymond Chandler

With an Introduction by Philip Durham

killer in the rain

raymond chandler

killer in the rain · Raymond Chandler

Houghton Mifflin Company

Raymond Chandler

Jacket design by
Rob Howard

Dust jacket for A 14.2

A 14.3
Third edition: New York: Pocket Books, [1965].

#75138. 75¢. Wrappers.

A 14.4
Fourth edition: [Harmondsworth]: Penguin/in association with Hamish Hamilton, [1966].

#C 2445. Wrappers. Reprinted 1969, 1971, 1973, 1976 (twice).

A 14.5
Fifth edition: New York: Ballantine, [1972].

#02665-9. 95¢. Wrappers. Not seen. Reprinted twice 1972–1977. Also reprinted in Canada by Ballantine, 1977.

A 15 CHANDLER BEFORE MARLOWE

A 15.1.a
First edition, first printing (1973)

CHANDLER ᴮᴱᶠᴼᴿᴱ

RAYMOND CHANDLER'S
EARLY PROSE AND POETRY,
1908-1912

MARLOWE

EDITED BY MATTHEW J. BRUCCOLI
FOREWORD BY JACQUES BARZUN

UNIVERSITY OF SOUTH CAROLINA PRESS
COLUMBIA, SOUTH CAROLINA

A 15.1.a: second, third, and fourth lines in red; 8⁷/₁₆″ × 5¹/₂″

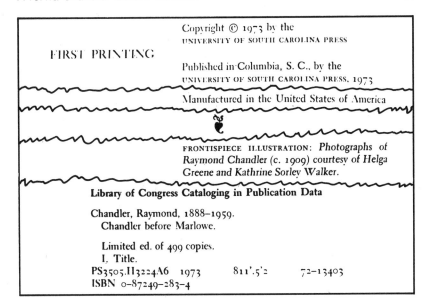

Copyright © 1973 by the
UNIVERSITY OF SOUTH CAROLINA PRESS

FIRST PRINTING

Published in Columbia, S. C., by the
UNIVERSITY OF SOUTH CAROLINA PRESS, 1973

Manufactured in the United States of America

FRONTISPIECE ILLUSTRATION: Photographs of Raymond Chandler (c. 1909) courtesy of Helga Greene and Kathrine Sorley Walker.

Library of Congress Cataloging in Publication Data

Chandler, Raymond, 1888–1959.
    Chandler before Marlowe.

    Limited ed. of 499 copies.
    I. Title.
PS3505.H3224A6   1973   811'.5'2   72–13403
ISBN 0–87249–283–4

Certificate of limitation: On free front endpaper:

'This is number [   ] of a limited first printing of four hun- | dred and ninety-nine copies of *Chandler Before Marlowe.* | Numbers 1 through 400 are for sale, and numbers 401 through | 499 have been distributed as complimentary copies to various | persons involved in the creation and the marketing of the book.

'*Chandler Before Marlowe* is printed on Warren's University | Text, a paper of extraordinary longevity, especially watermarked | with the emblem of the University of South Carolina Press. The | type was composed by Heritage Printers, primarily in Linotype | Electra of the 11-point size set on 13-point slugs. Display type | was set in Goudy Old Style with the exception of the one line of | Ultra Bodoni on the title page. After letterpress printing by | Heritage, the book was bound by the Carolina Ruling and | Binding Company in a three-piece binding of Kivar 9 Corin- | thian on the spine and Elephant Hide paper on the sides. The | binding materials were positioned by hand and butted one | against the other to prevent overlapping.

'This book contains reproductions of two previously unpub- | lished photographs of Raymond Chandler.

'The formal publication date of this book is 2 July 1973.

'The designer was Robert L. Nance.'

[A–B] [i–v] vi–xvii [xviii] [1–2] 3–51 [52–54] 55–81 [82–84] 85–96 [97–98] 99–101 [102–104] 105 [106–108] 109 [110]; tissue inserted between pp. ii and iii.

[1]⁸ (1₁ + 1) [2–8]⁸

Contents: p. A: half title; p. B: blank; p. i: photo of Chandler; p. ii: photo of Chandler; p. iii: title page; p. iv: copyright page; p. v: dedication; pp. vi–viii: contents; pp. ix–xii: 'THE YOUNG | RAYMOND | CHANDLER | JACQUES BARZUN'; pp. xiii–xvii: 'EDITOR'S | PREFACE | MATTHEW J. | BRUCCOLI'; p. xviii: blank; p. 1: section title for verse; p. 2: blank; pp. 3–51: text; p. 52: blank; p. 53: section title for essays and sketches; p. 54: blank; pp. 55–81: text; p. 82: blank; p. 83: section title for reviews; p. 84: blank; pp. 85–96: text; p. 97: section title for 'Chandler After Marlowe'; p. 98:

blank; pp. 99–101: text; p. 102: blank; p. 103: section title: 'Endnotes'; p. 104: blank; p. 105: text; p. 106: blank; p. 107: section title for 'Textual Notes'; p. 108: blank; p. 109: text; p. 110: blank.

42 pieces: "The Unknown Love," "The Poet's Knowledge," "The Soul's Defiance," "The Wheel," "Art," "A Woman's Way," "The Quest," "When I Was King," "The Hour of Chaos," "The Bed of Roses," "The Reformer," "The Perfect Knight," "A Pilgrim in Meditation," "The Pioneer," "The Hermit," "The Dancer," "The Death of the King," "The Clay God," "A Lament for Youth," "The Unseen Planets," "The Tears That Sweeten Woe," "The Fairy King," "Arise, ye phantoms of delight . . ." (untitled), "An Old House," "The King," "Time Shall Not Die," "Organ Music," "The Genteel Artist," "The Remarkable Hero," "The Literary Fop," "Realism and Fairyland," "The Tropical Romance," "Houses to Let," "The Phrasemaker," "The Rose-Leaf Romance," review of *The Broad Highway,* review of *The Reason Why,* "The Art of Loving and Dying," "The Rural Labourer at Home," "Requiem," "Sonnet 13" (working draft), "Sonnet 13" (final draft). See B 13, C 1–C 39.

Typography and paper: See certificate of limitation.

Binding: Gray yellow (#90) paper-covered boards with deep reddish brown (#41) coated paper, shelfback; front, spine, and back goldstamped: Front: ' *"The obsessive character of his thought, which gives the novels | much of their power, is right here, full force, in these youthful | pages, so happily gathered and restored to our inquisitive but sym- | pathetic glance."* | —JACQUES BARZUN' [lower left: blindstamped USC Press device]'. Spine: 'CHANDLER BEFORE MARLOWE BRUCCOLI SOUTH CAROLINA'. Back: ' *"Man is too often nobler than his fate."* ' Endpapers of same paper as covers; certificate of limitation on free front endpaper. All edges trimmed and stained red. Black cloth bookmark ribbon. Black bands at top and bottom. Deep reddish brown coated-paper slipcase. See certificate of limitation.

Publication: 499 copies of the first printing. Published 2 July 1973. $25.00. Copyright 2 July 1973. Copyright #A453349.

Printing: See certificate of limitation.

Locations: Kent; LC (JUL 26 1973); Lilly.

A 15.1.b
First edition, second printing: Columbia: University of South Carolina Press, [1973].

Copyright page: 'Second Printing, July 1973'.

$4.95. Omits photos of Chandler and adds "Chandler Checklist," pp. 107–109.

A 16 THE BLUE DAHLIA

A 16.1.a
First edition, first printing (1976)

Raymond Chandler

The Blue Dahlia

A Screenplay

With a Memoir by John Houseman

Edited, with an Afterword
by Matthew J. Bruccoli

Southern Illinois University Press
Carbondale and Edwardsville

Feffer & Simons, Inc.
London and Amsterdam

A 16.1.a: $8^{15}/_{16}'' \times 6''$

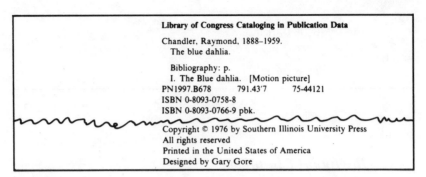

Library of Congress Cataloging in Publication Data

Chandler, Raymond, 1888–1959.
The blue dahlia.

Bibliography: p.
I. The Blue dahlia. [Motion picture]
PN1997.B678   791.43'7   75-44121
ISBN 0-8093-0758-8
ISBN 0-8093-0766-9 pbk.

Copyright © 1976 by Southern Illinois University Press
All rights reserved
Printed in the United States of America
Designed by Gary Gore

Clothbound

[A–B] [i–viii] ix–xxi [xxii–xxiv] [1–2] 3–139 [140–142]; 4 leaves of glossy illustrations inserted between pp. 58 and 59.

[1–2]¹⁶ [3–4]¹⁰ [5–6]¹⁶

Contents: pp. A–B: blank; p. i: SIU Press device; p. ii: photo of Chandler; p. iii: title page; p. iv: copyright page; p. v: 'Acknowledgments'; p. vi: blank; p. vii: 'Contents'; p. viii: blank; pp. ix–xxi: 'Lost Fortnight | *A Memoir* by John Houseman'; p. xxii: blank; p. xxiii: 'Editorial Note'; p. xxiv: blank; p. 1: script title; p. 2: 'Cast of Characters'; pp. 3–128: text, headed: 'MR Additional Scene'; pp. 129–137: 'Afterword | Raymond Chandler and Hollywood | By Matthew J. Bruccoli'; pp. 138–139: 'Appendix'; pp. 140–142: blank. See F4.

Typography and paper: 6³/₄″ (7¹/₂″) × 4¹/₈″. Running heads: versos, 'The Blue Dahlia | *A Screenplay*'. Wove paper.

Binding: Dark greenish blue (#174) V cloth (smooth). Front printed in dark blue with part of the screenplay. Spine silverstamped: '[vertical] Raymond Chandler The Blue Dahlia [2 lines, above] Southern Illinois [below] University Press'. Black endpapers. All edges trimmed. Black and white bands at top and bottom.

Dust jacket: Front is reproduction of movie poster within white border: '[yellow] ALAN LADD | VERONICA LAKE | WILLIAM BENDIX | [illustration of Bendix, Ladd, Lake, and, in lower left, Doris Dowling] | [light blue outlined in white with dark blue shadow] "THE | BLUE DAHLIA" | [red] a GEORGE MARSHALL production [dark blue Paramount seal] | [dark blue] [6 lines of credits]'. Spine: '[vertical] [against white] [black] Raymond Chandler [blue] The Blue Dahlia [gray SIU Press device]'. Back: '[against medium blue, within white single-rules frame] [white] Raymond | Chandler | [black] The Blue | Dahlia | [white] *A Screenplay* [black revolver] | [black] With a Memoir | by John Houseman | Edited, with an Afterword | by Matthew J. Bruccoli | [below frame] ISBN 0-8093-0758-8'. Front flap: blurb. Back flap: continuation of blurb and notes on Houseman and Bruccoli.

Publication: Published simultaneously in cloth and paper. 1,000 clothbound copies published 14 June 1976. $10.00. Copyright 21 June 1976. Copyright #A750713.

Printing: Composition, printing, and binding by the Colonial Press, Clinton, Mass.

Locations: LC (JUN 21 1976); Kent (dj).

Paperbound

Same pagination as clothbound. Perfect binding.

Dust jacket for A.16.1.a

Contents: Same as clothbound.

Typography and paper: Same as clothbound.

Binding: Stiff printed paper wrappers; same as dust jacket of clothbound, except that ISBN on back is '0-8093-0766-9'.

Publication: Published simultaneously in cloth and paper. 3,000 paperbound copies published 14 June 1976. $3.95.

Printing: Same as clothbound.

Location: Kent.

Review copy

Proof sheets bound in unprinted stiff white covers with white plastic comb binding. Two labels pasted on front: '[top label] [black] The Blue Dahlia'; '[bottom label] [on cream SIU Press letterhead] [black] THE BLUE DAHLIA | A Screenplay by Raymond Chandler | With a Memoir by John Houseman | Edited with an Afterword by Matthew J. Bruccoli | To be published by Southern Illinois University Press | April 26, 1976 | [underlined] uncorrected galley proof'.

Location: MJB.

A 16.1.b
First edition, first English printing (1976)

Raymond Chandler

The Blue Dahlia

A Screenplay

With a Memoir by John Houseman

Edited, with an Afterword
by Matthew J. Bruccoli

ELM TREE BOOKS
Hamish Hamilton · London

A 16.1.b: 9¹/₈″ × 6¹/₁₆″

Copyright page: 'First published in Great Britain 1976 | by Elm Tree Books Ltd | 90 Great Russell Street, London WCI | Copyright © by Southern Illinois University Press | SBN 241 89281 3 | Designed by Gary Gore | Printed in Great Britain by Ebenezer Baylis & Son Ltd | The Trinity Press, Worcester, and London'.

Same pagination as Southern Illinois University Press printing; 4 leaves of glossy illustrations inserted betwen pp. 70 and 71.

[1–4]¹⁶ [5]⁴ [6]¹⁶

Contents: Same as Southern Illinois Press printing, except that p. i substitutes half title for SIU device.

Typography and paper: Same as Southern Illinois University Press printing.

Binding: Strong red (#12) paper-covered boards with V grain. Spine goldstamped: '[vertical] Raymond Chandler The Blue Dahlia | [horizontal Elm Tree device]'. White endpapers. All edges trimmed.

Dust jacket: Same as Southern Illinois University Press printing, except for spine: '[vertical] [black] Raymond Chandler [blue] The Blue Dahlia | [horizontal] [black] [Elm Tree device] | ELM TREE BOOKS'. New copy on flaps.

Publication: Unknown number of copies of the first English printing. Published 16 September 1976. £3.95.

Printing: See copyright page.

Locations: BL (11 AUG 76); MJB (dj).

A 16.1.c
First edition, third printing (paper): Carbondale & Edwardsville: Southern Illinois University Press, [1976].

Copyright page: 'Second printing, August 1976'.

Part of this printing was distributed by the Quality Paperback Club.

A 16.1.d
First edition, fourth printing (cloth): Carbondale & Edwardsville: Southern Illinois University Press, [1977].

Copyright page: 'Second printing, January 1977'.

Note   ·

The Blue Dahlia was fictionalized by David Fraser, *Screen Romances,* 28 (June 1946), 34–37, 75–80.

A 17 THE NOTEBOOKS

A 17.1.a
First edition, first printing (1976)

The Notebooks of Raymond Chandler

and

English Summer

A Gothic Romance

by Raymond Chandler

Illustrated by Edward Gorey

Edited by Frank MacShane

The Ecco Press / New York

A 17.1.a: 9³/₁₆″ × 6³/₁₆″

Copyright © Helga Greene for the Estate of Raymond Chandler, 1976

All rights reserved

First published in 1976 by Ecco Press
1 West 30th Street, New York, N.Y. 10001

Published simultaneously in Canada by The Macmillan Company
of Canada Limited

Library of Congress Cataloging in Publication Data
Chandler, Raymond, 1888-1959.
The notebooks of Raymond Chandler and English summer, a gothic romance.
I. Chandler, Raymond, 1888-1959. English summer. 1976. II. Title.
PS3505.H3224A6   1976   813'.5'2   76-3322
ISBN 0-912-94633-4

Printed in the United States of America

Acknowledgments:

Antaeus: "A Qualified Farewell" (appeared in *Antaeus* under the title "Fare-
well, My Hollywood") and *English Summer, a Gothic Romance*, by Raymond
Chandler, Copyright © 1976 by Antaeus, New York, N.Y. The Atlantic
Monthly: from the review by Raymond Chandler, "The Hollywood Bowl,"
Copyright © 1946 by The Atlantic Monthly Company, Boston, Mass.; reprinted
with permission. Doubleday & Company, Inc., and the Estate of W. Somerset
Maugham and William Heinemann Ltd.: from *The Summing Up* by W.
Somerset Maugham, Copyright 1938 by W. Somerset Maugham; reprinted by
permission. E. P. Dutton & Co., Inc.: from *The Life of Raymond Chandler* by
Frank MacShane, Copyright © 1976 by Frank MacShane; reprinted by permis-
sion of the publishers, E. P. Dutton & Co., Inc. Holt, Rinehart and Winston,
Publishers: from *Writing Is Work* by Mary Roberts Rinehart, which origi-
nally appeared in The Saturday Evening Post, Copyright © 1939 by Curtis
Publishing Company; reprinted by permission of Holt, Rinehart and Winston,
Publishers. Houghton Mifflin Company and Hamish Hamilton Ltd.: from
Raymond Chandler Speaking, edited by Dorothy Gardiner and Kathrine
Sorley Walker (1962). Hope Leresche & Sayle: from *Mr. Fortune Objects* by
H. C. Bailey. Liveright Publishing Corporation: from *Crimes of the Year* by
Joseph Gollimb. Los Angeles Times: from *Town Called Hollywood* by Philip
K. Scheuer, Copyright 1936, Los Angeles Times; reprinted by permission. The
Saturday Evening Post: from "Pickpocket Lingo," Copyright 1950, The Curtis
Publishing Company; from "Beyond Disgust," Copyright 1941, The Curtis
Publishing Company; from "Railroad Slang," Copyright 1937, The Curtis
Publishing Company; all reprinted with permission from The Saturday Even-
ing Post. Scott Meredith Literary Agency, Inc.: from "Some Notes on Mystery
Novels and Their Authors," by Frank Gruber; reprinted by permission of Mrs.
Lois Gruber and Agents for the Estate of Frank Gruber, Scott Meredith
Literary Agency, Inc., 845 Third Avenue, New York, N.Y. 10022. The Sunday
Times (London): from "Bonded Goods" by Raymond Chandler.

Book design: Samuel N. Antupit

[i–x] 1–3 [4–6] 7–76 [77–87] 88–113 [114–118]

[1–4]^{16}

Contents: pp. i–ii: blank; p. iii: title page; p. iv: copyright page; p. v: contents; p. vi:
blank; p. vii: continuation of contents; p. viii: blank; p. ix: half title; p. x: blank; pp. 1–3:
foreword by Frank MacShane; p. 4: blank; p. 5: section title; p. 6: blank; pp. 7–113:
text; pp. 114–118: blank.

The Notebooks: "Great Thought," "Notes on 'Writing Down,' " "Since All Plans Are
Foolish . . . ," "Titles," "Descriptive Note," "Jack Woodford's Rules for Writing a
Novel," "Beyond Disgust," "Descriptions of Women," "Fashion Notes—Men," "Story
Idea: Fantastic," "Narration," "In Defense of the Classics," "Beginning of an Essay,"
"Notes (very brief, please) on English and American Style," "Beer in the Sergeant
Major's Hat," "A Routine to Shock the Neighbours: Is It Any Wonder?" "Lines to a Lady
with an Unsplit Infinitive," "A Defense of Impurity," "Some Notes on Mystery Novels

and Their Authors," "Twelve Notes on the Mystery Story," "Story Idea: Revenge," "Mary Roberts Rinehart on the Crime Novel," "Bonded Goods," "Song at Parting," "The Tragedy of King Richard III," "Chandlerisms," "A Routine to Shock the Neighbours: Faster, Slower, Neither," "Railroad Slang," "Slang and Hard Talk," "Note on the Tommy Gun," "San Quentin Prison Slang," "Craps," "Pickpocket Lingo," "Note on Typewriter Ribbon Code Dating," "Similes and Comparisons," "The Hollywood Bowl," "Some Rare Cooked Viands," "A Qualified Farewell," "The Scrapbook," "English Summer." See A 13, C 68, C 88, C 102, C 103.

Typography and paper: 7³/₈″ (7⁷/₈″) × 4³/₈″; 44 lines per page. No running heads. Wove paper.

Binding: Dark purplish red (#259) V cloth (smooth). Spine goldstamped: '[vertical] The Notebooks of Raymond Chandler English Summer by Raymond Chandler | [horizontal] ECCO'. Strong red endpapers. Top and bottom edges trimmed. Red and white bands at top and bottom.

Dust jacket: Front, spine, and back against tan background. Front: '[on orange page of loose-leaf binder] The | Notebooks | Of | Raymond | Chandler | [on green page of book] English | Summer | A Gothic Romance | by | Raymond | Chandler'. Spine: '[vertical] [on orange page of loose-leaf binder] The Notebooks of Raymond Chandler [on green page of book] English Summer by Raymond Chandler | [horizontal] Ecco'. Back: continuation of orange page of loose-leaf binder above green page of *English Summer;* at lower left: 'SBN: 912-94633-4'. Front flap: blurb. Back flap: '[red] *Other Books by The Ecco Press:* [9 titles]'.

Publication: 6,108 copies of the first printing. Published 1 December 1976. $10.00. Copyright 1 November 1976. Copyright #A830772.

Printing: Composed, printed, and bound by the Vail-Ballou Press, Binghampton, N.Y.

Locations: Kent (dj); LC (FEB 22 1977); Lilly (dj).

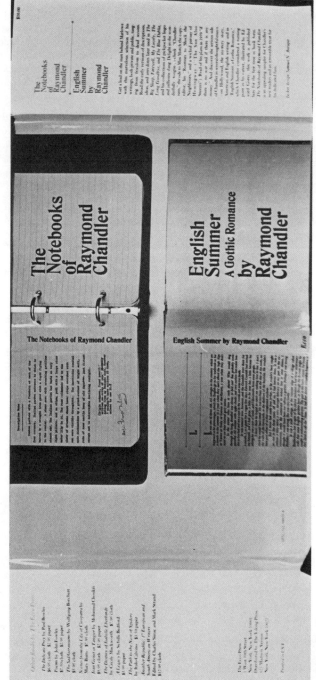

Dust jacket for 17.1.a

A 17.1.b
First edition, first English printing (1977)

The Notebooks of Raymond Chandler

and

English Summer

A Gothic Romance

by Raymond Chandler

Illustrated by Edward Gorey

Edited by Frank MacShane

Weidenfeld and Nicolson · London

A 17.1.b: 6¹/₁₆″ × 9¹/₈″

Copyright page: 'Copyright © 1976 by Helga Greene for the | Estate of Raymond Chandler | First published in Great Britain by | Weidenfeld and Nicolson | 11 St John's Hill London SW 11 | 1977 | [7 lines of type] | ISBN 0 297 77430 1 | Printed in Great Britain by | REDWOOD BURN LIMITED | Trowbridge & Esher'.

Same pagination as Ecco printing.

[1–8]⁸

Contents: Same as Ecco printing.

Typography and paper: Same as Ecco printing.

Binding: Dark red (#16) paper-covered boards with C (sand grain) pattern. Spine goldstamped: '[vertically within single-rule frame] The Notebooks of Raymond Chandler [diamond] English Summer by Raymond Chandler Weidenfeld | & Nicolson'. White endpapers. All edges trimmed.

Dust jacket: Front: '[all against mottled red and white background, which is continued on spine and back] [on white panel within black single-rule frame] [black] The Notebooks of | [blue] RAYMOND | CHANDLER | [black rule decorated with red diamonds] | [black] and | [blue] English Summer | [black] A Gothic Romance by | Raymond Chandler'. Spine: '[vertically on white panel within single-rule black frame] [black] The Notebooks of [blue] Raymond Chandler [red diamond] [black] English Summer by [blue] Raymond Chandler [black] Weidenfeld | & Nicolson'. Back: '[on white panel within black single-rule frame] [blue] CHANDLERISMS | [black rule decorated with red diamonds] [12 excerpts from *Notebooks* in black, blue, and red]'. Front flap has blurb for the book. Back flap has ad for *The World of Raymond Chandler.*

Publication: Unknown number of copies of the first English printing. Published 24 October 1977. £4.50.

Printing: See copyright page.

Locations: BL (17 OCT 77); MJB.

A 18 CHANDLER/FOX LETTERS
Forthcoming (1978)

Letters Raymond Chandler and James M. Fox, ed. James Pepper. Santa Barbara, Cal.: Neville-Yellin, 1978.

350 numbered copies, 26 lettered copies, and 30 presentation copies. All copies signed by James M. Fox.

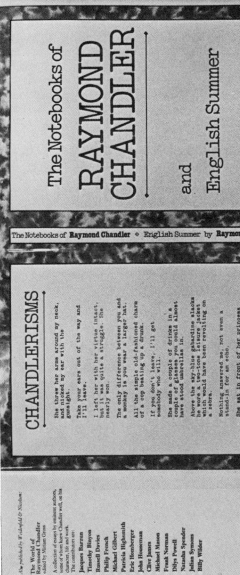

Get a load on the man behind Marlowe with this characteristic selection of this writings collected here for the first time in book form. Read the early versions of descriptions, ideas, and anecdotes later used in *The Big Sleep*, *Farewell, My Lovely*, *The Long Goodbye*, and *The Blue Dahlia*, and his collection of pickpocket lingo and jailhouse slang. Delight in the wonderfully tongue-in-cheek 'Chandlerisms', the ode to Miss Muriel the copy-editor, his 'Routines to Shock the Neighbours', and a wicked parody of Hemingway ('The Sun Also Sneezes'). Read of his plain in 1939: 'if there is no war and if there is any money?'

Discover, too, the serious side of Chandler in several thoughtful essays—on Hollywood, the mystery story, American and English writing—and in *English Summer: A Gothic Romance* which Chandler considered a turning point in his career; it is illustrated by Edward Gorey.

The Notebooks of Raymond Chandler is an appealing sampler for Chandler's new readers and an irresistible treat for his dedicated fans.

£4.50 net
UK ONLY

The Notebooks of RAYMOND CHANDLER

and

English Summer

A Gothic Romance by Raymond Chandler

The Notebooks of **Raymond Chandler** ◇ English Summer by **Raymond Chandler**   Weidenfeld & Nicolson

CHANDLERISMS

She threw her arms around my neck, and nicked my ear with the gunsight.

Take your ears out of the way and I'll leave.

I left her with her virtue intact, but it was quite a struggle. She nearly won.

The only difference between you and a monkey is you wear a larger hat.

All the simple old-fashioned charm of a cop beating up a drunk.

If you don't leave, I'll get somebody who will.

She made a couple of drinks in a couple of glasses you could almost have stood umbrellas in.

Above the sky-blue gabardine slacks he wore a two-tone leisure jacket which would have been revolting on a zebra.

Nothing answered me, not even a stand-in for an echo.

She sat in front of her princess dresser trying to paint her eyes, suitcases out from under her eyes.

The boys who talk and spit without ever bothering the cigarettes that live in their faces.

Goodnight, goodbye and I'd hate to be you.

Also published by Weidenfeld & Nicolson:

The World of Raymond Chandler edited by Miriam Gross

A collection of essays by eminent authors, some of whom knew Chandler well, on his character, life and work. The contributors are:

Jacques Barzun
Timothy Binyon
Russell Davies
Philip French
Michael Gilbert
Patricia Highsmith
Eric Homberger
John Houseman
Clive James
Michael Mason
Frank Norman
Dilys Powell
Natasha Spender
Julian Symons
Billy Wilder

Weidenfeld and Nicolson
11 St John's Hill London SW11

ISBN 0 297 77450 1

Dust jacket for A 17.1.b

AA. Supplement

Collections

AA 1 RAYMOND CHANDLER'S MYSTERY OMNIBUS

AA 1.1.a

RAYMOND CHANDLER'S | *Mystery Omnibus* | *Containing THE BIG SLEEP* | *and FAREWELL, MY LOVELY* | [Forum Books device] CLEVELAND AND NEW YORK | *THE WORLD PUBLISHING COMPANY*

[1944].

On copyright page: 'FORUM BOOKS EDITION | *First Printing June 1944*'.

No first book material. See A 1.5.a, A 2.4.a.

Paper-covered boards; dust jacket. $1.00.

AA 1.1.b
Second printing: Cleveland & New York: World, [1945].

On copyright page: 'Second Printing June 1945'.

AA 2 RED WIND

RAYMOND CHANDLER | Red Wind | *A Collection of Short Stories* | [rule] | [Tower Books device] CLEVELAND AND NEW YORK | THE WORLD PUBLISHING COMPANY

[1946].

On copyright page: 'Published by THE WORLD PUBLISHING COMPANY | 2231 WEST 110TH STREET • CLEVELAND 2 • OHIO | *By arrangement with Raymond Chandler* | TOWER BOOKS EDITION | *First Printing March 1946* | HC | COPYRIGHT 1946 BY THE WORLD PUBLISHING COMPANY | MANUFACTURED IN THE UNITED STATES OF AMERICA'.

5 stories: "Red Wind," "Blackmailers Don't Shoot," "I'll Be Waiting," "Goldfish," "Guns at Cyrano's." *No first book material.* See A 5, A 6, C 40, C 46, C 49, C 55, C 61.

Paper-covered boards; dust jacket. 49¢.

AA 3 SPANISH BLOOD

Spanish Blood | *A COLLECTION OF SHORT STORIES* | by RAYMOND CHANDLER | [Tower Books device] | THE WORLD PUBLISHING COMPANY | *CLEVELAND AND NEW YORK*

[1946].

On copyright page: 'Published by THE WORLD PUBLISHING COMPANY | 2231 WEST 110TH STREET • CLEVELAND 2 • OHIO | *By arrangement with Mr. Raymond Chandler* | TOWER BOOKS EDITION | *First Printing July 1946* | HC | COPYRIGHT 1946 BY THE WORLD PUBLISHING COMPANY | MANUFACTURED IN THE UNITED STATES OF AMERICA'.

5 stories: "Spanish Blood," "The King in Yellow," "Pearls Are a Nuisance," "Nevada Gas," "Trouble Is My Business." *No first book material.* See A 5, A 6, C 44, C 45, C 56, C 59, C 60.

Paper-covered boards; dust jacket. $1.00.

AA 4 TROUBLE IS MY BUSINESS

AA 4.1

RAYMOND CHANDLER | *Trouble is my Business* | AND OTHER STORIES | PENGUIN BOOKS | HARMONDSWORTH • MIDDLESEX

[1950].

5 stories: "Trouble Is My Business," "Red Wind," "I'll Be Waiting," "Goldfish," "Guns at Cyrano's." *No first book material.* See A 5, A 6, C 46, C 49, C 55, C 60, C 61.

#741. 1/6. Wrappers. Reprinted 1951, 1952, 1954, 1957, 1960.

AA 4.2
Second edition: [Harmondsworth]: Penguin, [1962].

#741. 3/6. Wrappers. Reprinted 1964, 1967, 1972, 1976.

AA 4.3
Third edition

RAYMOND CHANDLER | [decorated rule] | TROUBLE IS | MY BUSINESS | • | *Four Stories from* | THE SIMPLE ART OF MURDER | [kangaroo] | POCKET BOOKS, INC., NEW YORK

[1951].

On copyright page: 'POCKET BOOK edition published November, 1951 | 1st printing . . . . October, 1951'.

4 stories: "Trouble Is My Business," "Finger Man," "Goldfish," "Red Wind." *No first book material.* See A 5, A 6, A 7, C 42, C 49, C 55, C 60.

#823. 25¢. Wrappers. 3 printings, 1951–1957.

AA 4.4
Fourth edition: New York: Ballantine, [1972].

Not seen. Reprinted twice 1972–1977. Also reprinted in Canada by Ballantine.

AA 5 PICK-UP ON NOON STREET

AA 5.1

Raymond Chandler | PICK-UP | ON NOON STREET | [rule] | FOUR STORIES FROM | THE SIMPLE ART OF MURDER | [kangaroo] | POCKET BOOKS, INC. • NEW YORK, N.Y.

[1952].

On copyright page: 'POCKET BOOK edition published February, 1952 | 1st printing . . . . January, 1952'.

4 stories: "Pick-Up on Noon Street," "Smart-Aleck Kill," "Guns at Cyrano's," "Nevada Gas." *No first book material.* See A 5, A 7, A 9, C 41, C 44, C 46, C 48.

#846. 25¢. Wrappers. 7 printings, 1925–1965.

AA 5.2
Second edition: London: Harborough, [1960].

4 stories: "Smart-Aleck Kill," "Pick-Up on Noon Street," "Nevada Gas," "Spanish Blood."

Ace #H308. 2/6. Wrappers.

AA 5.3
Third edition: New York: Ballantine, 1972.

Not seen. Reprinted twice 1972–1977. Also reprinted in Canada by Ballantine, 1977.

AA 6 RAYMOND CHANDLER OMNIBUS

AA 6.1

THE | RAYMOND | CHANDLER | OMNIBUS | [hh device] | HAMISH HAMILTON | LONDON

[1953].

On copyright page: '*The Raymond Chandler Omnibus* was first published in 1953 by Hamish Hamilton Ltd. . . .'

4 novels: *The Big Sleep; Farewell, My Lovely; The High Window; The Lady in the Lake. No first book material.* See A 1.10, A 2.7, A 3.6, A 4.7.

15s. Paper-covered boards; dust jacket. 5 printings, 1953–1964.

AA 6.2
Second edition: London: Companion Book Club, [1963]. 11s.

AA 7 SMART-ALECK KILL

AA 7.1

SMART-ALECK KILL | By | RAYMOND CHANDLER | [hh device] | HAMISH HAMILTON | LONDON

[1953].

On copyright page: '*First published in Great Britain in 1953. . . .*'

4 stories: "Smart-Aleck Kill," "Pick-Up on Noon Street," "Nevada Gas," "Spanish Blood." *No first book material.* See A 5, A 7, A 9, C 41, C 44, C 45, C 48.

2s. Wrappers.

Reprinted in hardbound format 1958, 1959, 1962.

AA 7.2

Second edition: [Harmondsworth]: Penguin/in association with Hamish Hamilton, [1964].

#C2198. 3/6. Wrappers. Reprinted 1969, 1972, 1976.

AA 8 PEARLS ARE A NUISANCE

AA 8.1

PEARLS ARE | A NUISANCE | By | RAYMOND CHANDLER | [hh device] | HAMISH HAMILTON | LONDON

[1958].

On copyright page: *'First published in this Edition in 1958. . . .'*

3 stories: "Introduction," "Pearls Are a Nuisance," "Finger Man," "The King in Yellow"; and "The Simple Art of Murder." *No first book material.* See A6, A7, A9, C42, C56, C59, C64, C76.

7/6. Paper-covered boards; dust jacket. Reprinted 1959, 1962.

AA 8.2

Second edition: [Harmondsworth]: Penguin/Hamish Hamilton, [1964].

#C2136. 3/6. Wrappers. Reprinted 1966, 1969, 1973, 1976.

AA 9 SECOND CHANDLER OMNIBUS

THE | SECOND | CHANDLER | OMNIBUS | [hh device] | HAMISH HAMILTON | LONDON

[1962].

On copyright page: 'The Second Chandler Omnibus was first published in 1962 by Hamish Hamilton Ltd. . . .'

3 novels: *The Little Sister, The Long Good-bye,* and *Playback;* and "The Simple Art of Murder." *No first book material.* See A7, A8.6, A10.7, A11.6, C64, C75, C76, C96.

25s. Paper-covered boards; dust jacket. Reprinted.

AA 10 RAYMOND CHANDLER OMNIBUS

[script] The [roman] RAYMOND | CHANDLER | OMNIBUS | [following 6 lines within decorated panel] FOUR FAMOUS CLASSICS | *The Big Sleep* | *Farewell, My Lovely* | *The High Window* | *The Lady in the Lake* | FOREWORD BY LAWRENCE CLARK POWELL | [following 2 lines within decorated panel] [borzoi device and 3 decorations] | NEW YORK [script] Alfred • A • Knopf [roman] 1964

On copyright page: 'FIRST COLLECTED EDITION'.

No first book material. See A1.12, A2.8, A3.7, A4.10.

$5.95. Clothbound; dust jacket. Reprinted 1969, 1975. Also distributed by The Book-of-the-Month Club and Quality Paperback Club.

AA 11 THE SMELL OF FEAR

AA 11.1.a

The Smell of Fear | By | RAYMOND CHANDLER | *comprising* | BLACKMAILERS DON'T SHOOT | PEARLS ARE A NUISANCE | FINGER MAN | THE KING IN YELLOW | SMART-ALECK KILL | PICK-UP ON NOON STREET | NEVADA GAS | SPANISH BLOOD | TROUBLE IS MY BUSINESS | RED WIND | I'LL BE WAITING | GOLDFISH | GUNS AT CYRANO'S | THE PENCIL | [hh device] | HAMISH HAMILTON | LONDON

[1965].

On copyright page: 'First published in Great Britain 1965. . . .'

Also includes "Introduction" by Chandler. *First book publication of* "The Pencil." See A 5, A 6, A 7, A 9, C 40–C 42, C 44, C 45, C 46, C 48, C 49, C 55, C 56, C 59–C 61, C 98.

30s. Paper-covered boards; dust jacket.

Location: BL (14 JUN 65).

Review copy

Book sheets in printed yellow paper wrappers.

Location: Kent.

AA 11.1.b
Second printing: London: Hamish Hamilton, [1973].

A Fingerprint Book. Reprinted 1977.

AA 12 MIDNIGHT RAYMOND CHANDLER

THE | MIDNIGHT | RAYMOND | CHANDLER | [rule] | *with an Introduction by* | JOAN KAHN | [device] | HOUGHTON MIFFLIN COMPANY BOSTON | 1971

On copyright page: 'First Printing C'.

5 stories and 2 novels: "The Simple Art of Murder," "Red Wind," "Trouble Is My Business," "Blackmailers Don't Shoot," "The Pencil," *The Little Sister, The Long Goodbye. No first book material.* See A 5, A 6, A 8.8, A 10.9, AA 11, C 40, C 55, C 60, C 75, C 76, C 98.

$10.00. Clothbound; dust jacket.

AA 13 OCTOPUS CHANDLER

The Big Sleep | The High Window | The Lady in the Lake | The Long Goodbye | Playback | Farewell My Lovely | Heinemann [slash] Octopus | [slanted] *Raymond* | *CHANDLER*

[1977].

No first book material. See A 1, A 2, A 3, A 4, A 10, A 11.

£4.95. Clothbound; dust jacket. Published jointly by Heinemann, Secker & Warburg, and Octopus Books.

B. First-Appearance Contributions to Books

B1 AVON STORY TELLER

[within double-rules frame] [script] The Avon | Story Teller | [head of Shakespeare] | [roman] New Avon Library | Jo Meyers • E. B. Williams | 119 West 57th Street New York 19

[1945]. New Avon Library #72.

"Pick-Up on Noon Street," pp. 24–76. See A 9, C 48.

B2 THIRD MYSTERY COMPANION

[within triple-rules frame] Third Mystery | Companion | *Edited by* | A. L. FURMAN | [fleuron] | GOLD LABEL BOOKS | New York

[1945].

"The Simple Art of Murder" (from *The Atlantic Monthly*), pp. 252–268. The unrevised version. See C 64.

B3 GREAT AMERICAN DETECTIVE STORIES

[2-page title] [left:] GREAT AMERICAN | *Stories by* CORNELL WOOLRICH • WILLIAM MAC HARG | DASHIELL HAMMETT • RAYMOND CHANDLER • CRAIG RICE | ANNA KATHARINE GREEN • MELVILLE DAVISSON POST | ANTHONY BOUCHER • ELLERY QUEEN • JACQUES FUTRELLE | STUART PALMER • FRANK GRUBER • T. S. STRIB-LING | ANTONIO HELÚ • PAUL GALLICO • EDGAR ALLAN POE • [right:] DETECTIVE STORIES | EDITED, WITH AN INTRODUCTION, | BY ANTHONY BOUCHER | CLEVE-LAND AND NEW YORK [tower seal] | THE WORLD PUBLISHING COMPANY

[1945].

On copyright page: 'AN ORIGINAL TOWER BOOKS PUBLICATION | *First Published June 1945*'.

"No Crime in the Mountains," pp. 49–95. See A 14, C 63.

B4 ART OF THE MYSTERY STORY

[within decorated-rules frame] THE ART OF THE | MYSTERY | STORY | A Collection of | Critical Essays | Edited and with a commentary by | HOWARD HAYCRAFT | [device] | SIMON AND SCHUSTER | New York • 1946

109

"The Simple Art of Murder" (from *The Atlantic Monthly*), pp. 222–237. "The version presented here was specially revised by Mr. Chandler for this publication." See A 7, C 64.

B 5 BEST FILM PLAYS

[decorated frame within single-rule frame] BEST FILM PLAYS | —1945 | *Edited by* | JOHN GASSNER | *and* DUDLEY NICHOLS | [device] | CROWN PUBLISHERS | NEW YORK

[1946].

Double Indemnity, screenplay by Chandler and Billy Wilder, pp. 115–174. See F 1.

B 6 HARD-BOILED OMNIBUS

The Hard-Boiled | *Omnibus* | ††† | EARLY STORIES | FROM *BLACK MASK* | †† | Edited and with an Introduction by | JOSEPH T. SHAW | † | [device] | SIMON AND SCHUSTER • NEW YORK

[1946].

"The Man Who Liked Dogs," pp. 112–156. See A 14, C 47.

B 7 TWENTIETH CENTURY AUTHORS

TWENTIETH CENTURY | AUTHORS | FIRST SUPPLEMENT | A Biographical Diction-ary of Modern Literature | *Edited by* | STANLEY J. KUNITZ | *Assistant Editor* | VINETA COLBY | [device] | NEW YORK | THE H. W. WILSON COMPANY | NINETEEN HUNDRED FIFTY-FIVE

Autobiographical sketch by Chandler, pp. 186–187.

B 8 FOR BOND LOVERS ONLY

B 8.1

FOR | BOND | LOVERS ONLY | [rule] | Compiled and Edited | by Sheldon Lane | [panther device] | A Panther Book

London, [1965]. #1941.

Donald Gomery, "Iced Water and Cool Customers," pp. 143–146. Interview. See C 95.

B 8.2
[New York]: Dell, [1965].
#2672.

B 9 BANG TO RIGHTS

FRANK NORMAN | [rule of diamonds] [letters of following 2 lines slanted] Bang to | Rights | [rule of diamonds] | AN ACCOUNT OF PRISON LIFE | *With a Foreword by* | RAYMOND CHANDLER | *London:* SECKER & WARBURG: 1958

"Foreword," p. 7. Also on front and back of dust jacket. See E 1.

B 10 IN FRIENDLY CANDOR

In Friendly Candor | *by* | EDWARD WEEKS | [Atlantic Monthly Press device] | *An Atlantic Monthly Press Book* | BOSTON • Little, Brown and Company • TORONTO

1959.

Letter to Weeks, pp. 285–286.

B 11 BOYS IN THE BLACK MASK

THE BOYS IN THE | [star] BLACK | MASK [star] | [left: man with revolver] [right: mask] AN EXHIBIT | IN THE | UCLA | LIBRARY | [below illustration:] January 6–February 10, 1961

Cover title.

Excerpts from 2 Chandler letters, p. 4.

B 12 DOWN THESE MEAN STREETS A MAN MUST GO

[2-page title] [left:] [seal] | CHAPEL HILL | THE UNIVERSITY OF NORTH CAROLINA PRESS | [right:] [following 3 lines against gray design probably intended to represent street intersection] DOWN THESE | MEAN STREETS | A MAN MUST GO | *Raymond Chandler's Knight* | BY PHILIP DURHAM

[1963].

First publication of letters and verse.

B 13 TUTTO MARLOWE INVESTIGATORE

Raymond Chandler | TUTTO MARLOWE | INVESTIGATORE | Il testimone | Il grande sonno | Addio, mia amata | Finestra sul vuoto | In fondo al lago | Con 12 illustrazioni | Nel testo | *volume primo* | (1934–1943) | ARNOLDO MONDADORI EDITORE

[1970].

On copyright page: 'I edizione Omnibus Gialli giugno 1970'.

Facsimile of revised typescript for "Sonnet 13," p. xxii; facsimile of manuscript for "Foreword" to *Bang to Rights*, p. xxiii. See A 15, B 9.

B 14 LIFE OF RAYMOND CHANDLER

B 14.1

[decorated rule] | THE | LIFE | OF | RAYMOND | CHANDLER | [decorated rule] Frank MacShane | [Dutton device] | E. P. DUTTON & CO., INC. | NEW YORK

[1976].

On copyright page: 'First Edition | 10 . . . 1'.

Material from letters, work in progress, notebooks.

B 14.2

London: Jonathan Cape, 1976.

B 15 WORLD OF RAYMOND CHANDLER

B 15.1

The World of | RAYMOND CHANDLER | [tapered rule] | Edited by Miriam Gross | *Introduction by Patricia Highsmith* | Weidenfeld and Nicolson | London

[1977].

Excerpts from letters.

B 15.2

New York: A&W, [1978].

C. First Appearances in Magazines and Newspapers

C 1
"The Rose-Leaf Romance," unlocated.

Story. See A 15.

C 2
"Organ Music," unlocated.

Poem. See A 15.

C 3
"The Unknown Love." *Chambers's Journal*, 12 (19 December 1908), 48.

Poem. See A 15.

C 4
"The Poet's Knowledge." *The Westminster Gazette*, 33 (3 March 1909), 2.

Poem. See A 15.

C 5
"The Soul's Defiance." *The Westminster Gazette*, 33 (5 March 1909), 2.

Poem. See A 15.

C 6
"The Wheel." *The Westminster Gazette*, 33 (26 March 1909), 2.

Poem. See A 15.

C 7
"Art." *The Westminster Gazette*, 33 (16 April 1909), 2.

Poem. See A 15.

C 8
"A Woman's Way." *The Westminster Gazette*, 33 (22 April 1909), 2.

Poem. See A 15.

C 9
"The Quest." *The Westminster Gazette*, 33 (2 June 1909), 2.

Poem. See A 15.

C 10
"When I Was King." *The Westminster Gazette*, 33 (9 June 1909), 2.

Poem. See A 15.

C 11
"The Hour of Chaos." *The Westminster Gazette,* 33 (18 June 1909), 2.

Poem. See A 15.

C 12
"The Bed of Roses." *The Westminster Gazette,* 33 (29 June 1909), 2.

Poem. See A 15.

C 13
"The Reformer." *The Westminster Gazette,* 34 (29 July 1909), 2.

Poem. See A 15.

C 14
"The Perfect Knight." *The Westminster Gazette,* 34 (30 September 1909), 2.

Poem. See A 15.

C 15
"A Pilgrim in Meditation." *The Westminster Gazette,* 34 (8 November 1909), 2.

Poem. See A 15.

C 16
"The Pioneer." *The Westminster Gazette,* 34 (17 November 1909), 2.

Poem. See A 15.

C 17
"The Hermit." *The Westminster Gazette,* 35 (28 February 1910), 2.

Poem. See A 15.

C 18
"The Dancer." *The Academy,* 78 (14 May 1910), 462.

Poem. See A 15.

C 19
"The Death of the King." *The Spectator,* 105 (16 July 1910), 97.

Poem. See A 15.

C 20
"The Clay God." *The Westminster Gazette,* 37 (4 January 1911), 2.

Poem. See A 15.

C 21
"A Lament for Youth." *The Westminster Gazette,* 37 (9 February 1911), 2.

Poem. See A 15.

C 22
Untitled review of *The Broad Highway* by Jeffery Farnol. *The Academy,* 80 (18 March 1911), 328–329.

Unsigned. See A 15.

C 23
"The Unseen Planets." *The Westminster Gazette,* 37 (21 April 1911), 2.

Poem. See A 15.

C 24
"The Tears That Sweeten Woe." *The Westminster Gazette,* 37 (1 May 1911), 2.

Poem. See A 15.

C 25
"The Fairy King." *The Westminster Gazette,* 36 (3 May 1911), 2.

Poem. See A 15.

C 26
Untitled poem, "Arise, ye phantoms of delight. . . ." *The Westminster Gazette,* 37 (16 June 1911), 2.

See A 15.

C 27
"The Genteel Artist." *The Academy,* 81 (19 August 1911), 250.

Essay. See A 15.

C 28
"The Remarkable Hero." *The Academy,* 81 (9 September 1911), 322.

Unsigned essay. See A 15.

C 29
"The Literary Fop." *The Academy,* 81 (4 November 1911), 560.

Essay. See A 15.

C 30
"An Old House." *The Westminster Gazette,* 38 (15 November 1911), 2.

Poem. See A 15.

C 31
Untitled review of *The Reason Why* by Elinor Glyn. *The Academy,* 81 (23 December 1911), 796–797.

Unsigned. See A 15.

C 32
"Realism and Fairyland." *The Academy,* 82 (6 January 1912), 5.

Essay. See A 15.

C 33
"The Tropical Romance." *The Academy,* 82 (20 January 1912), 84.

Essay. See A 15.

C 34
"Houses to Let." *The Academy,* 82 (24 February 1912), 248–249.

Essay. See A 15.

C 35
"The King." *The Westminster Gazette,* 39 (1 March 1912), 2.
Poem. See A 15.

C 36
"Time Shall Not Die." *The Westminster Gazette,* 39 (25 April 1912), 2.
Poem. See A 15.

C 37
"The Art of Loving and Dying." *The Academy,* 82 (22 June 1912), 774–775.
Unsigned review of *The Drama of Love and Death* by Edward Carpenter. See A 15.

C 38
"The Rural Labourer at Home." *The Academy,* 82 (22 June 1912), 776–777.
Unsigned review of *Change in the Village* by George Bourne. See A 15.

C 39
"The Phrasemaker." *The Academy,* 82 (29 June 1912), 817–818.
Essay. See A 15.

C 40
"Blackmailers Don't Shoot." *Black Mask,* 16 (December 1933), 8–35.
Story. Syndicated by King Features, April 1947.
See A 5.

C 41
"Smart-Aleck Kill." *Black Mask,* 17 (July 1934), 54–78.
Story. See A 7.

C 42
"Finger Man." *Black Mask,* 17 (October 1934), 8–38.
Story. See A 7.

C 43
"Killer in the Rain." *Black Mask,* 17 (January 1935), 8–33.
Story. See A 14.

C 44
"Nevada Gas." *Black Mask,* 18 (June 1935), 8–34.
Story. Syndicated by King Features, July 1946. See A 5.

C 45
"Spanish Blood." *Black Mask,* 18 (November 1935), 38–64.
Story. Syndicated by King Features, April 1947. See A 5.

C 46
"Guns at Cyrano's." *Black Mask*, 18 (January 1936), 8–37.

Story. Syndicated by King Features, April 1947. See A 5.

C 47
"The Man Who Liked Dogs." *Black Mask*, 19 (March 1936), 10–33.

Story. See A 14, B 6.

C 48
"Noon Street Nemesis." *Detective Fiction Weekly*, 102 (30 May 1936), 36–62.

Story. Retitled "Pick-Up on Noon Street." See A 9, B 1.

C 49
"Goldfish." *Black Mask*, 19 (June 1936), 10–35.

Story. Syndicated by King Features, April 1947. See A 5.

C 50
"The Curtain." *Black Mask*, 19 (September 1936), 10–33.

Story. See A 14.

C 51
"Try the Girl." *Black Mask*, 19 (January 1937), 10–34.

Story. See A 14.

C 52
"A Letter About the Article on Floral Arrangement. . . ." *The Fortnightly Intruder*, 2 (15 June 1937), 5–6.

C 53
"A Second Letter from R. C. Esq. . . ." *The Fortnightly Intruder*, 2 (1 July 1937), 6–7.

C 54
"Mandarin's Jade." *Dime Detective*, 25 (November 1937), 36–67.

Story. See A 14.

C 55
"Red Wind." *Dime Detective*, 26 (January 1938), 40–70.

Story. Syndicated by King Features, December 1947. See A 6.

C 56
"The King in Yellow." *Dime Detective*, 26 (March 1938), 42–74.

Story. See A 6.

C 57
"Bay City Blues." *Dime Detective*, 27 (June 1938), 6–47.

Story. See A 14.

C 58

"The Lady in the Lake." *Dime Detective,* 29 (January 1939), 94–127.

Story. See A 14.

C 59

"Pearls Are a Nuisance." *Dime Detective,* 30 (April 1939), 68–96.

Story. See A 6.

C 60

"Trouble Is My Business." *Dime Detective,* 31 (August 1939), 42–76.

Story. See A 6.

C 61

"I'll Be Waiting." *The Saturday Evening Post,* 212 (14 December 1939), 10–11, 72, 74–75, 78.

Story. See A 6.

C 62

"The Bronze Door." *Unknown,* 11 (November 1939), 90–106.

Story. See A 7.

C 63

"No Crime in the Mountains." *Detective Story,* 162 (September 1941), 9–54.

Story. See A 14, B 3.

C 64

"The Simple Art of Murder." *The Atlantic Monthly,* 174 (December 1944), 53–59.

Article. There are 2 articles titled "The Simple Art of Murder." The *Atlantic* article is longer and begins, "The detective story . . . ." *The Saturday Review of Literature* article (C 76) begins, "As a writer . . . ." The *Atlantic* article was revised in 1946 for *The Art of the Mystery Story* (B 4) and was included in that form in *The Simple Art of Murder* (1950) (A 9). The *Saturday Review* article was revised as the "Introduction" to *The Simple Art of Murder.* See also B 2.

C 65

"Writers in Hollywood." *The Atlantic Monthly,* 176 (November 1945), 50–54.

Article. See A 13.

C 66

Wallace, Irving. "He Makes Murder Pay." *Pageant,* 2 (July 1946), 126–129.

Interview.

C 67

"Author of Big Sleep Succumbs to La Jolla." *San Diego Journal* (1946).

Interview.

C 68

"The Hollywood Bowl." *The Atlantic Monthly,* 179 (January 1947), 108–109.

Review of *The Golden Egg* by James S. Pollack. See A 17.

C 69
" 'Pros' and Cons——." *Harper's Magazine,* 194 (May 1947), xiii.

Letter.

C 70
Nolan, Terry. "Air Fare: Chandler Likes Radio IF: 'Philip Marlowe' Variable." *San Diego Journal* (1 July 1947), p. 12.

Interview.

C 71
"Critical Notes." *The Screen Writer,* 3 (July 1947), 31–32.

C 72
"Oscar Night in Hollywood." *The Atlantic Monthly,* 181 (March 1948), 24–27.

Article.

C 73
"Studies in Extinction." *The Atlantic Monthly,* 181 (April 1948), 110–112.

Review of *Murders Plain and Fanciful* by James Sandoe.

C 74
"10 Greatest Crimes of the Century." *Cosmopolitan,* 125 (October 1948), 50–53.

Article.

C 75
"The Little Sister." *Cosmopolitan,* 126 (April 1949), 173–196.

Prepublication abridgement. See A 8.

C 76
"The Simple Art of Murder." *The Saturday Review of Literature,* 33 (15 April 1950), 13–14.

Article. Reprinted as "Introduction" to *The Simple Art of Murder.* See A 9, C 64.

C 77
Letter to the editor. *The Author,* 61 (Spring 1951), 93–94.

C 78
"Professor Bingo's Snuff." *Park East,* 11 (June 1951), 14–15, 52–54; (July 1951), 29, 52–54; (August 1951), 27, 52–55.

Story. Also appeared in *Go* (June–July 1951), pp. 81–93. Priority undetermined.

C 79
"Ten Per Cent of Your Life." *The Atlantic Monthly,* 189 (February 1952), 48–51.

Article. See A 13.

C 80
Autobiographical note. *Fantastic,* 1 (Summer 1952), inside front wrapper.

C 81
Ray, Cyril. "The Unconventional Mr. Chandler Comes to Town." *London Sunday Times* (21 September 1952), p. 8.

Interview.

C 82
Forster, Peter. "Gentle Tough Guy." *John O'London's Weekly,* 62 (6 March 1953), 189.

Interview.

C 83
Starrett, Vincent. "Books Alive." *Chicago Sunday Tribune* (10 April 1955), sec. 4, p. 4.

Interview.

C 84
MacColl, Rene. "Raymond Chandler Now Says I Confess . . . ." *London Daily Express* (25 April 1955), p. 6.

Interview. See Appendix 1.

C 85
"Ruth Ellis—Should She Hang?" *London Evening Standard* (30 June 1955), p. 5.

Letter.

C 86
"A Letter from London." *The Third Degree,* 11 (September/October 1955), 3–4.

C 87
Winn, Merrick. "A Confession by Raymond Chandler." *London Daily Express* (14 January 1956), p. 4.

Interview.

C 88
"Bonded Goods." *London Sunday Times* (25 March 1956), p. 7.

Review of *Diamonds Are Forever* by Ian Fleming. See A 17.

C 89
"Crosstown with Neil Morgan." *San Diego Evening Tribune* (1 March 1957).

Guest column.

C 90
"Raymond Chandler writes a blunt letter to the Daily Express." *London Daily Express* (25 May 1957), p. 3.

Letter.

C 91
"A Star Writer's Advice to Writers (and editors)." *London Daily Express* (18 June 1957), p. 4.

Letter.

C 92
"Crosstown with Neil Morgan." *San Diego Evening Tribune* (12 July 1957).

Guest column.

C 93
"Crosstown with Neil Morgan." *San Diego Evening Tribune* (8 March 1958).

Letter.

C 94
"The Terrible Dr. No." *London Sunday Times* (30 March 1958), p. 6.

Review of *Dr. No* by Ian Fleming.

C 95
Gomery, Donald. "Raymond Chandler Talks of James Bond . . . ." *London Daily Express* (7 July 1958), p. 4.

Interview. See B 8.

C 96
"Playback." *Suspense,* 1 (October 1958), 130–160; (November 1958), 126–160.

Also appeared in *Personality* (4 December 1958), pp. 76–77, 97–105; (18 December 1958), pp. 64–69; (1 January 1959), pp. 50–54, 65–70; (15 January 1959), pp. 42–45. See A 11, F 7.

C 97
"The Detective Story as an Art Form." *The Crime Writer,* 9 (Spring 1959), 5.

Article.

C 97a
"MWA Loses Its President." *The Crime Writer,* 9 (Spring 1959), 5, 18.

Chandler's remarks on being elected president of the Mystery Writers of America.

C 98
"Marlowe Takes on the Syndicate." *London Daily Mail* (6 April 1959), p. 4; (7 April), p. 4; (8 April), p. 8; (9 April), p. 4; (10 April), p. 4.

Story. Abridged in *Perth Daily News* (15 May 1959), p. 6; (16 May), p. 6; (18 May), p. 6; (19 May), p. 6; (20 May), p. 6. Full text appeared as "Wrong Pigeon," *Manhunt,* 8 (February 1969), 1–27. Also appeared as "The Pencil," *Argosy,* 26 (September 1965), 126–159, and "Philip Marlowe's Last Case," *Ellery Queen's Mystery Magazine,* 39 (January 1962), 30–43, 84–96. See AA 11, AA 12.

C 99
"Crosstown with Neil Morgan." *San Diego Evening Tribune* (25–26 August 1959).

Posthumously published guest column in two parts.

C 100
Fleming, Ian. "Raymond Chandler." *London Magazine,* 6 (December 1959), 43–54.

Includes letters.

C 101
"Private Eye." *London Sunday Times* (25 February 1962), p. 28.

Prepublication excerpts from *Raymond Chandler Speaking*. Also appeared as "Private Eye in a World of Letters," *New York Herald Tribune Book Review* (11 March 1962), p. 3.

C 102
"Farewell, My Hollywood." *Antaeus*, 21/22 (Spring/Summer 1976), 24–33.

Article. Reprinted in A 17 as "A Qualified Farewell."

C 103
"English Summer." *Antaeus*, 23 (Autumn 1976), 7–27.

Story. See A 17.

D. Keepsake

D 1

CHANDLER | ON PROOF READING | [Penguin device] January 1963

[1–4]

[1]²

Cover title. 5⁷/₈″ × 3⁹/₁₆″.

Excerpts Chandler's 18 January 1948 letter to Edward Weeks.

Privately printed by the Merrian Press, London. Probably 6 copies on deep reddish orange (#36) paper and 30 copies on yellow gray (#93) paper

Location: Kent (orange and gray).

CHANDLER
ON PROOF READING

 January 1963

D 1, cover title: 5⁷/₈″ × 3⁹/₁₆″

E. Dust-Jacket Blurbs

E 1

See *Bang to Rights* (1958). B 9.

E 2

Atlee, Philip. *The Irish Beauty Contract*. Greenwich, Conn.: Fawcett Gold Medal, [1966].

#D1976. Blurb on front wrapper and last page.

F. Motion-Picture Work

F 1
Double Indemnity. Paramount, 1944.

Screenplay by Chandler and Billy Wilder from the novel by James M. Cain. Screenplay received Academy Award nomination. Directed by Billy Wilder; produced by Joseph Sistrom. Featured Fred MacMurray, Barbara Stanwyck, and Edward G. Robinson. See B 5.

F 2
And Now Tomorrow. Paramount, 1944.

Screenplay by Chandler and Frank Partos from the novel by Rachel Field. Directed by Irving Pichel, produced by Fred Kohlmar. Featured Alan Ladd and Loretta Young.

F 3

The Unseen. Paramount, 1945.

Screenplay by Chandler and Hagar Wilde; adapted by Wilde and Ken Englund from *Her Heart in Her Throat* by Ethel Lina White. Directed by Lewis Allen; produced by John Houseman. Featured Joel McCrea, Gail Russell, and Herbert Marshall.

F 4
The Blue Dahlia. Paramount, 1946.

Screenplay by Chandler from his original screen story. Screenplay received Academy Award nomination. Directed by George Marshall; produced by John Houseman. Featured Alan Ladd, Veronica Lake, and William Bendix. See A 16.

F 5
Strangers on a Train. Warner Brothers, 1951.

Screenplay by Chandler and Czenzi Ormonde; adapted from the Patricia Highsmith novel by Whitfield Cook. Directed and produced by Alfred Hitchcock. Featured Farley Granger, Ruth Roman, and Robert Walker.

UNPRODUCED SCREENPLAY ASSIGNMENTS

F 6
The Innocent Mrs. Duff. Paramount, 1946.

From the novel by Elisabeth Sanxay Holding.

135

F 7
Playback. Universal, 1947–1948.

From Chandler's original story. Converted into a novel. See A 11, C 96.

MOTION PICTURES MADE FROM CHANDLER'S BOOKS

F 8
The Falcon Takes Over. RKO, 1941.

Screenplay by Lynn Root and Frank Fenton from *Farewell, My Lovely* (and the Michael Arlen character).

F 9
Time to Kill. Twentieth Century–Fox, 1942.

Screenplay by Clarence Upson Young from *The High Window* (and Brett Halliday's Michael Shayne character).

F 10
Murder, My Sweet. RKO, 1945.

Screenplay by John Paxton from *Farewell, My Lovely.*

F 11
The Big Sleep. Warner Brothers, 1946.

Screenplay by William Faulkner, Leigh Brackett, and Jules Furthman.

F 12
The Lady in the Lake. MGM, 1946.

Screenplay by Steve Fisher. Chandler worked on the script, but withdrew and refused screen credit.

F 13
The Brasher Dubloon. Twentieth Century–Fox, 1947.

Screenplay by Dorothy Hannah; adapted by Leonard Praskins from *The High Window.*

F 14
Marlowe. MGM, 1969.

Screenplay by Stirling Silliphant from *The Little Sister.*

F 15
The Long Goodbye. United Artists, 1974.

Screenplay by Leigh Brackett.

F 16
Farewell, My Lovely. Avco Embassy, 1976.

Screenplay by David Z. Goodman.

F 17
The.Big Sleep. United Artists, 1978.

Screenplay by Michael Winner.

Appendices / Index

Appendix 1

Compiler's Notes

" 'After I left Dulwich I went to work on the Daily Express as a reporter. I was a complete flop. Every time they sent me out on a story I would get lost. They fired me. I deserved it.' " Rene MacColl, "Raymond Chandler Now Says I Confess . . . ," *London Daily Express* (25 April 1955), p. 6.

" 'I used to do mostly paragraphs (which I lifted from foreign language papers) for the *Westminster Gazette* and verses and sketches.' " *Twentieth Century Authors: First Supplement,* ed. Stanley J. Kunitz (New York: Wilson, 1955), p. 186.

". . . upon returning to Los Angeles in 1919, he took a position on the *Daily Express,* but stayed for only six weeks." Frank MacShane, *The Life of Raymond Chandler* (New York: Dutton, 1976), p. 31.

Appendix 2

Principal Works About Chandler

[Durham, Philip.] *The Boys in the Black Mask.* [Los Angeles: UCLA Library, 1961]. See B 11.

Durham, Philip. *Down These Mean Streets a Man Must Go.* Chapel Hill: University of North Carolina Press, 1963. See B 12.

MacShane, Frank. *The Life of Raymond Chandler.* New York: Dutton, 1976; London: Cape, 1976. See B 14.

Pendo, Stephen. *Raymond Chandler: His Novels Into Film.* Metuchen, N.J.: Scarecrow Press, 1976.

Sandoe, James. *The Hard-Boiled Dick: A Personal Checklist.* Chicago: Lovell, 1952.

Index

Powell, Lawrence Clark, A 1.12, A 2.8,
A 3.7, A 4.10, AA 10
Praskins, Leonard, F 13
Priestley, J. B., A 8.1.a
"Private Eye," C 101
"Private Eye in a World of Letters," C 101
"Professor Bingo's Snuff," C 78
" 'Pros' and Cons——," C 69
"The Publication of Raymond Chandler's
The Long Goodbye," A 10.1.a
Pyramid Books, A 11.7

"A Qualified Farewell," A 17, C 102
Quality Book Club, A 14.1.c
Quality Paperback Club, A 16.1.c, AA 10
Queen, Ellery, B 3
"The Quest," A 15, C 9

"Railroad Slang," A 17
Ray, Cyril, C 81
"Raymond Chandler," C 100
Raymond Chandler: His Novels Into Film,
App. 2
"Raymond Chandler and Hollywood," A 16
"Raymond Chandler Now Says I
Confess . . . ," C 84, App. 1
The Raymond Chandler Omnibus (London), A 1.10, A 2.7, A 3.6, A 4.7, AA 6
The Raymond Chandler Omnibus (New
York), A 1.12, A 2.8, A 3.7, A 4.10, AA 10
Raymond Chandler on Writing, A 12
Raymond Chandler's Mystery Omnibus,
A 1.5.a, A 2.4.a, AA 1
Raymond Chandler Speaking, A 12, A 13,
C 101
"Raymond Chandler Talks of James
Bond . . . ," C 95
"Raymond Chandler writes a blunt letter
to the Daily Express," C 90
Reading-For-Men, A 10.4
"Realism and Fairyland," A 15, C 32
The Reason Why, A 15, C 31
Red Wind, AA 2
"Red Wind," A 6, A 9.1.a, AA 2, AA 4.1,
AA 4.3, AA 11, AA 12, C 55
"The Reformer," A 15, C 13
"The Remarkable Hero," A 15, C 28
"Requiem," A 15
Rice, Craig, B 3
RKO, F 8, F 10
Robinson, Edward G., F 1
Roman, Ruth, F 5
Root, Lynn, F 8
"The Rose-Leaf Romance," A 15, C 1
"A Routine to Shock the Neighbours: Is It
Any Wonder?" A 17
"A Routine to Shock the Neighbours:
Faster, Slower, Neither," A 17

"The Rural Labourer at Home," A 15, C 38
Russell, Gail, F 3
"Ruth Ellis—Should She Hang?" C 85

San Diego Evening Tribune, C 89, C 92,
C 93, C 99
San Diego Journal, C 67, C 70
Sandoe, James, C 73, App. 2
"San Quentin Prison Slang," A 17
The Saturday Evening Post, C 61
The Saturday Review of Literature, C 64,
C 76
Scarecrow Press, App. 2
"The Scrapbook," A 17
Screen Romances, note following
A 16.1.d
The Screen Writer, C 71
Secker & Warburg, AA 13, B 9
The Second Chandler Omnibus, A 8.6,
A 10.7, A 11.6, AA 9
"A Second Letter from R. C. Esq . . . . ,"
C 53
Shaw, Joseph Thompson, A 5, B 6
Silliphant, Stirling, F 14
"Similes and Comparisons," A 17
Simon & Schuster, A 1.11, B 4, B 6
The Simple Art of Murder, A 9, C 64, C 76
"The Simple Art of Murder," A 7, A 9,
AA 8, AA 9, AA 12, B 2, B 4, C 64, C 76
"Since All Plans Are Foolish . . . ," A 17.
See also "1939 Plan of Work Taken
from Chandler's Notebooks"
Sistrom, Joseph, F 1
"Slang and Hard Talk," A 17
Smart-Aleck Kill, AA 7
"Smart-Aleck Kill," A 7, A 9.1, A 9.2,
AA 5.1, AA 5.2, AA 7, AA 11, C 41
The Smell of Fear, AA 11
"Some Notes on Mystery Novels and
Their Authors," A 17
"Some Rare Cooked Viands," A 17
"Song at Parting," A 17
"Sonnet 13" (final draft), A 15
"Sonnet 13" (revised typescript), A 15,
B 13
"The Soul's Defiance," A 15, C 5
Southern Illinois University Press,
A 16.1.a, A 16.1.c, A 16.1.d
Spanish Blood, AA 3
"Spanish Blood," A 5, A 9, AA 3, AA 5.2,
AA 7, AA 11, C 45
The Spectator, C 19
Stanwyck, Barbara, F 1
Star Editions, A 8.1.c
Starrett, Vincent, C 83
"A Star Writer's Advice to Writers (and
editors)," C 91

Pittsburgh Series in Bibliography